Biedermeier Furniture

Library bookcase, cherry with apple, 270 x 275 x 69 cm. Southwest German, circa 1820. Value over $30,000. Dr. Nagel, Stuttgart.

Biedermeier Furniture

Rudolf Pressler & Robin Straub

77 Lower Valley Road, Atglen, PA 19310

Cover photo:
Sofa, mahogany on softwood, with maple stripe inlays and ornamented mahogany inlays in maple fields, 93.5 x 211 x 69 cm. Berlin, circa 1825, Joachim Mayer, Göttingen.

Back cover:
Tea table and set of four chairs circa 1825 (see F 20 on page 83) Karin Streminski, Cologne.

Library of Congress Cataloging-in-Publication Data

Pressler, Rudolf.
    [Biedermeier-Möbel. English]
    Biedermeier furniture/Rudolf Pressler & Robin Straub.
       p.   cm.
    Includes bibliographical references.
    ISBN 0-7643-0155-1 (hbk.)
    1. Furniture--Austria--History--19th century--Catalogs.
    2. Decoration and ornament--Austria--Biedermeier style--Catalogs.
    3. Furniture--Germany--History--19th century--Catalogs.
    4. Decoration and ornament--Germany--Biedermeier style--Catalogs.
    I. Straub, Robin. II. Title.
    NK2544.P7413   1996
    749.2'36'09034075--dc20
                          96-28956
                          CIP

Printed in the United States of America

ISBN: 0-7643-0155-1

1996 Book Design by Michael William Potts.

Published by Schiffer Publishing, Ltd.
77 Lower Valley Road
Atglen, PA 19310
Phone: (610) 593-1777
Fax: (610) 593-2002

Please write for a free catalog.
This book may be purchased from the publisher.
Please include $2.95 for shipping.
Try your bookstore first.

We are interested in hearing from authors with book ideas on related subjects.

Contents

INTRODUCTION TO THE STYLE

ILLUSTRATIONS

GALLERY OF ILLUSTRATIONS

Foreword

There previously has been very little literature that deals exclusively with the furniture of the Biedermeier era in Austria and Germany, 1815 to 1848, and no single book that provides the student of antique furniture with a catalog of the style with price comparisons. Thus this book will surely fill a gap in the available literature on the subject.

This book is oriented completely to practical use, including a large illustration section that shows exclusively furniture that has been sold in recent years. The introduction is meant to bring the historical surroundings of the Biedermeier era into closer understanding by the antiquary and collector. Here the furniture is shown to be an expression of the living culture of the epoch and simultaneously the reflection of a social structure in transition, in which the contours of our present times were already taking shape. In this respect, Biedermeier is presented as a typically German culture based style. Advice and encouragement for collecting in general, as well as for the collecting of Biedermeier furniture in particular, are offered, so that this book will serve as a handbook for professionals and enthusiasts alike.

The two authors are members of the Stuttgart auction house of Dr. Nagel. Through their daily contact with antiques, including those from the first half of the nineteenth century, they were aware of the need for such a reference work. In the end, it just took many "overtime hours and night shifts" to produce the book that lies before you.

The Values

The price listings should be regarded merely as a guide, and the value to the true aficionado must be disregarded. Surely a reader will encounter a lack of cooperation when, in the course of purchasing negotiations for a particularly well-proportioned secretary, which fits precisely into the space on the purchaser's wall, he tries to drive down the price by referring to a generally similar piece shown in this book. Direct comparisons are only possible within limits, and thus the stated values should be no more than points of reference, though they should be definite enough to offer protection from serious purchasing errors and completely unrealistic expectations.

Acknowledgments

In order to make the factual material in the text as reliable as possible, the authors were able to gain the cooperation of the Augsburg restorer Uwe Dobler for the chapters "Maintaining Value by Restoration and Care" and "Design" of Biedermeier furniture. He has gained a fine reputation through the numerous jobs that he has done and continues to do in the service of great museums. The publishers and authors would like to take this opportunity to express their thanks to him for his willingness to add his profound knowledge to this book.

The publisher also thanks Rita Bucheit of Rita Bucheit, Ltd. Fine Arts & Antiques in Chicago for assistance with some of the furniture terminology in English. Her keen knowledge of the style and technical terms is appreciated.

Introduction

"Biedermeier":
A Caricature gives the Time its Name

"Once upon a time there was . . ." — thus could this chapter begin, and one would surely add something thereby to the further understanding of a very misunderstood epoch. For the down-to-earth sound of the name "Biedermeier" often enough turns out to be the cause of a false conception of the period between the Congress of Vienna in 1815 and the Revolution in Germany of 1848.

To understand the word "Biedermeier" we must first know its origin in literature. It was in this era that the Grimm Brothers published their pedagogically intended fairy tales, and in 1844 Dr. Heinrich Hoffmann, a physician, published his cartoon book "Slovenly Peter". So: Once upon a time . . . the subsequent painter-poet Josef Viktor von Scheffel, who, at the age of 22 in 1848, published poems with such titles as "Biedermann's Evening Socializing" and "Bummelmaier's Complaint" in the *Flying Leaves*, a weekly paper founded in 1844 by Kaspar Braun and Friedrich Schneider. Thanks to the founders' good-natured humor, the paper was typically cynical in character.

The names of von Scheffel's characters "Biedermann" and "Bummelmaier" were combined by publisher Ludwig Eichrodt in his pseudonym "Gottlieb Biedermaier", under which he, along with his friend, the physician Adolf Kussmaul, published the poems of a naive village schoolmaster Samuel Friedrich Sauter, in which they disclosed the culmination of "pleasant domesticity".

As yet, "Biedermaier" was still spelled with "ai". Only in 1869 did Eichrodt publish "Biedermeiers Liederlust" and help the presently customary spelling become established. In this form, the cynical ideas expressed in the writings were taken up by the younger generation and linked to the low opinion with which one is often inclined to judge the old and the out-of-fashion. Looking back, one saw in Mr. "Biedermeier" only the small man satisfied to live a simple life of simple pleasures, withdrawing inside his own four walls and singing Sauter's "Potato Song" in praise of the Creator of the potato. This, to be sure, is not true to the life style of the period from 1815 to 1848. It only serves to explain the origin of the term "Biedermeier."

As an era in art history, "Biedermeier" did not become recognized until about 1900 when it was realized that the art created in the first half of the nineteenth century in Germany possesses characteristics that set it apart clearly from the previous Empire style and the subsequent Historicism.

Surely it would have been convenient if the art-historical concept of Biedermeier had been limited to the period still characterized today in Germany as "Vormärz". But its roots are found in the late eighteenth century and its influence extends far beyond the revolutionary year of 1848. Therefore, the Biedermeier concept breaks into two aspects, namely a cultural-historical one, such as was expressed by Max von Böhn in his book *Biedermeier, Deutschland 1815-1847*, and an art-historical one, first introduced by Richard Hamann in 1914 in his work *German Painting in the 19th Century*.

The volume at hand deals with a portion of the art-historical Biedermeier, but an introduction to the living conditions of the time and their origins would appear to be urgently needed in a book about Biedermeier furniture. We are speaking here of the most intimate expression of Biedermeier culture. The Biedermeier furniture presently serves as a document of a private philosophy of life, which placed great value on domesticity. Let us try to get into the world of Mr. Biedermeier's thoughts and feelings.

At the Congress of Vienna in 1815, the opportunity to develop a single German state was rejected under the leadership of Prince von Metternich. Instead, the German Bund was prescribed as an absolutely ruled feudal system of small states. Power was returned, without limits, to the hands of the monarchs, and this took place after the people had, for the first time, been able to develop a feeling of togetherness by combining into a single German speaking army to fight against Napoleon. Together with the concepts of freedom that came out of the French Revolution, the middle class developed a new self-awareness that was badly stifled by the final decisions in Vienna after the Austrian state chancellor made himself into the leading European statesman in the interests of the Habsburgs. Sarcastic names like "Prince von Midnight" or "State Hemorrhoidarius" are only a few examples of the mood of the common people at the time, which was expressed in the student movements that began in Jena and Giessen and peaked at the Wartburg Festival with its call for German unity. The assassination of the dramatist Kotzebue, suspected of being a Russian agent, by the student Karl Ludwig Sand, gave the absolute rulers a very welcome excuse to build up a system of surveillance and spying. Thus critical comments in a letter read by the censors could result in years of imprisonment for the author. Under the repressive climate of the "Karlsbad Decrees", which called for persecution of demagogues and the banning of fraternities, political life came to an almost complete standstill. As a result, Mr. "Biedermeier" withdrew into private life and took pleasure in the small things nearest to him. In 1816, approximately ninety per-cent of the population lived in the country, in the simplest of conditions. Traveling was done only in overfilled mail coaches, made even more difficult by hours of waiting for the horses to be changed and stopping at every toll station. Weights, measures and coinage were not equitable. The cities, lacking light in their streets, looked as medieval as ever. In Berlin in 1826, the first gas streetlights were installed, and a 10:00 P.M. curfew was prescribed. Sewage flowed in open ditches next to the sidewalks. Since there was scarcely a bathroom or kitchen with running water, one had to fetch buckets of water from a public pump. The example of sending a letter will show how difficult, even in the first half of the nineteenth century, things were that we take for granted today. There was no united postal system, and no postage stamps. Envelopes were unknown. One had to pick up a wax-sealed letter at the post office and pay the postage for it there.

The (1) isolation of the individual communities, as well as the (2) stated social conditions, together with the (3) political repression constituted the three essential factors of the Biedermeier life style of the middle class. The conditions strengthened after the Wars of Liberation until 1830 to encourage the people to withdraw into themselves, and the period is now satirized as being full of kitsch. The resulting simplicity of life was well suited to the prevailing artistic style, which was already suggested in Goethe's *Hermann und Dorothea*: "Everything is simple and smooth: carved work and gilding are no longer wanted."

In the evening, when people sat around the table together in the light of the tallow candles trimmed with candle-snuffers, many people were present. In addition to the family with its numerous children and grandparents, the maid was also taken into the circle, as well as the hired men and apprentices, if the father was an artisan. Sociability was nurtured in a small group without much extension. People exchanged invitations, drank herb tea, and pieces of literature were often read.

Clothing fashions changed very little during the "Vormärz" period. The man wore a tailcoat, a colorful vest and drainpipe trousers, and on his head was a top hat of felt. Neckties were to be tied so that only the corners of the "patricide" collar could be seen. The "Frau" — only the nobility were so addressed; otherwise one said "Madame" — dressed herself in a figure-fitting tunic-like dress with puffed or leg-of-mutton sleeves. The length of the dress left the foot and sometimes the ankle joint uncovered, and one could see the lace-trimmed garments worn underneath. Her head was adorned with a bonnet or similar hat preserved in slightly changed form from the eighteenth century.

A change in the philosophy of privacy, when the sewing table and the *servante* — that piece of furniture which the housewife adorned with her modest collection of knick-knacks — as symbols of the pleasure found in the small and simple, came about in the year 1830.

Knowing as he did that the effect of restorative powers in France had achieved only moderate success, Charles X resorted to the method of the coup-d'etat. He abolished the freedom of the press, changed the right of suffrage, and dissolved the congress. Just days later, the July Revolution broke out, at the end of which the Duke of Orléans was enthroned as Louis Philippe I, the so-called Citizen King. The predominance of the middle class was based on the form of the constitutional-parliamentary monarchy.

The events in France naturally had their effect on the middle class self-image in Germany. The Hambach Festival of 1832 was a high point in the fight for more freedom and the unity of Germany. Technical novelties and industrial developments allowed the middle class's wish for a unified market to become more and more urgent. On January 1, 1834 the German Customs Union was founded, with eighteen German states as members who no longer had to pay customs duties to each other. When they could move their merchandise more easily, the merchants' productive powers could develop more freely. With that, the Biedermeier era began to decline in both its cultural-historical and its art-historical sense.

Finally, traveling became simpler, thanks to an increasingly better-developed network of roads and railroads. Ideas could be exchanged beyond the local boundaries; the horizon expanded. Even the particularly stringent intervention of the powers of "Restoration" — as the period between the Congress of Vienna (1815) and the March Revolution (1848), the era of Metternich, is called — could not change that. To be sure, the political leaders, by using their united powers in the Restoration era, tried to do away with German reforms and restore the "old order", and even C. L. von Haller's work of political theory, *Restoration of the Sciences of State*, could not prevent the fall of the old order in 1848. The human and spiritual potential that had developed between 1815 and 1830 within its own four walls was too great; the course of history could no longer be held back.

In any case, the formation of the school system and the creation of the teaching profession count as great achievements of the Biedermeier era. Before that, the schoolmasters were artisans, soldiers or student dropouts who provided the students entrusted to them with only the barest necessities of reading and writing ability. Only after the first half of the nineteenth century has the process of training capable instructors been in existence. In the higher schools, the dominance of Latin was replaced by a more all-around education and the Abitur examination introduced as a prerequisite for university study. Research was ranked more highly than theory in higher education, and the development of individual intellectual achievements was promoted. All of these reforms were based on the Biedermeier principle of educating one's offspring appropriately for its age. Thus "the family in the Biedermeier age has truly been a well-protected world of the child" (Doderer, Biedermeier).

The "pure Biedermeier" will therefore only be found in the first fifteen years of this style period, when social life outside the family took place only in the south German taverns or wine bars. In Berlin, the pastry shops served as the centers of communication, for newspapers were available there, as also in the Viennese coffee houses. In the *Tabagien*, the beer bars of the simpler people, smoking was allowed, which was generally forbidden on the city streets until 1848. The only external sign of advancing liberalism was the growth of chin-whiskers after 1830. Until then, Mr. Biedermeier was clean-shaven, for a moustache was regarded as improper. Only with the approach of the Revolution was the full beard no longer regarded as plebeian.

Some statistics of industrial development illuminate the situation: in 1830 there were 245 steam engines in operation in Prussia, in 1837 there were already 419, and their numbers increased quickly, as did the number of workingmen as well: at the beginning of the thirties, there were 450,000, in the revolution year of 1848 there were already a million. All of these aspects scarcely portray the Biedermeier age as an idyllic period. Instead there were years of enormous economic, social and political changes, which culminated in the discharging and exile of Metternich in the March Revolution, the impetus for which came once again from

France. Shortly before, the February Revolution led to the flight of the Citizen King, who had clung too closely to the Metternich system.

It is almost like historical irony that the middle class sensitivity of the French resulted first in the fall of one of Metternich's followers and then finally the end of Metternich's own career. But as said above, this was only the spark that flashed from France to Germany; the groundwork for the Revolution had already been laid in 1830.

The Biedermeier Furniture Style

Origin

In order to understand the art of Biedermeier furniture in its totality, it is necessary to take a brief look back at the previous style epochs: the Louis XVI style that prevailed in the last third of the eighteenth century and the Empire style that reigned in the first fifteen years of the nineteenth century. This span of time, along with the subsequent thirty years of Biedermeier, generally has its artistic forms of expression labeled as Classicism. As different as the elegant, court-influenced Louis XVI style, the monumental Empire style limited exclusively to the reign of Napoleon, and the homey, middle class Biedermeier style may seem to us at first glance, all three of these distinct styles of Classicism, with all their specific characteristics, grew from the same roots in the history of art — the antique style. It must be kept in mind that, as in all stylistic changes over the centuries, the new is unthinkable without knowing what came before it, whether in terms of the adoption and further development of what was already at hand, or in the consequent rejection of the old, linked with the longing for a new spirit of life and new means of artistic expression.

And thus the Louis XVI style too, developing in France and striving for cubic completeness and variety of antique-style decorative elements, must be seen as a reaction to the playfulness of the Rococo, with its dissolution of overall form and its asymmetrical, naturalistic ornamentation. On the one hand, it was a desire for more domesticity and thus more privacy, away from the courtly and ceremonial, on the other hand, an artistic rediscovery of antique beauty of form as a result of the excavations at Herculaneum (1738) and Pompeii (1755).

It was the French architects who took up this new tendency and worked it out in the spirit of the times when they were commissioned to design German residences in the 1750-1760 period, thus setting the first tones in Germany. But Winckelmann too, himself an archaeologist, gained through his writings an influence, that cannot be overlooked, on the German development of clear architectural forms in combination with antique-style ornamentation. Despite the willingness of architects to accept the new forms, the furniture builders of Germany reacted hesitantly — with the exception of the Roentgen studio — to the new demands.

Unlike the situation in France, where there was a clearly recognizable transitional style from Rococo to Louis XVI, the German furniture designers, often limited by the reactionary guilds, held fast to the Rococo until about 1770, and to the Rococo style of interior decoration almost until the end of the eighteenth century. Was it, as F. Luthmer calls it, "the compelling German need for colorful content", or the economic and political difficulties that impelled a hasty arrival of Louis XVI style and inspired so many well-known designers such as Bennemann, Schwerdtfeger and Weisweiler to migrate to nearby France? When one looks at the new, style-setting pieces from this initial phase after 1770, one sees that their architectural appearance is strictly regulated, with columns and broad friezes, richly decorated with vases, festoons, staffs of pearls, meandering stripes and other antique decorative elements. This furniture is weighty, with rich and powerful decor, usually set off in white and gold.

The Queue style

The Queue style, still ridiculed at the beginning of the nineteenth century as the essence of everything old-fashioned, and later rehabilitated as the art-historical label for the German version of the Louis XVI style, only found a home east of the Rhine after 1780 and developed its defining structure and stylistic features.

It was the British model primarily that the harmonious Queue style was supposed to follow, for a development toward Classicism had already begun there, including in furniture building, in the late eighteenth century. The striving for greater functionality and fidelity to the material, which resulted in the creation of furniture in the sense of a new straightforwardness and comfort, was represented there from 1770 on, primarily by the architect Robert Adam. But Hepplewhite too, in his pattern book *The Cabinet-Maker's and Upholsterer's Guide*, and Thomas Sheraton, in *The Cabinet Maker's and Upholsterer's Drawing Book*, represented the new direction, at the end of the eighties and the beginning of the nineties, with designs for excellent furniture with emphasis on practical use.

Mobility was sought, so various new types of furniture such as worktables, etageres, and toilette cabinets with complicated interior layouts now found acceptance in home furnishings. Cylinder bureaus, with interesting mechanical complexity, and many other changeable pieces enjoyed great popularity.

In furniture made for sitting, the pierced chair back offered an area for working in decorative elements such as urns, vases, lyres and other antique motifs. New directions were also presented by the mahogany imported from overseas colonies and used almost exclusively, because of its strength and solid, firm structure. Used flat and massive or veneered and darkly polished, it afforded furniture a worthy elegance which was often emphasized by light and sometimes contoured inlays.

Otto Wagner (1803-1861), **Salon in a castle in 1850,** *watercolor, Peter Griebert Gallery, Grünwald near Munich.*

This furniture, depicted in the publications with pattern drawings that now appeared in greater and greater numbers on the continent — probably the most important and trend-setting, and well worth mentioning, was the *Journal of Luxury and Fashion* published in Weimar beginning in 1785 — inspired the imagination of German furniture makers.

Then too, the direct furniture imports of the north German coastlands, traditionally associated in trade with Britain, increased considerably, and many of the furniture makers now designated themseles as "English chairmaker", probably to make capital on the new markets and popular styles.

Thus David Roentgen, probably the most outstanding furniture artist of the queue style, liked to call himself and "English Cabinet-maker", as is documented on the occasion of a furniture lottery in Hamburg in about 1768. In this respect, David Roentgen must be regarded as the leader of this last style of the eighteenth century. Educated by numerous foreign travels, he understood, as did no other, how to subordinate the inlay as surface decoration and the bronze attachments as three-dimensional decor to the requirements of clarity in the antique-oriented style of Classicism.

At that time there appeared a multitude of small furniture items, such as worktables and bottle coolers oriented to domestic life and meeting the requirements of mobility and usefulness. The highly prized cylinder bureau and other writing tables were equipped with mechanical features unique in furniture building. Chairs with their pierced backs stressed lightness that also characterized commodes, half-chests and tables. This is furniture that is enlivened by the natural beauty and careful choice of woods and features simplicity and elegance.

The Queue style in Germany, the late Classical style in England, and the Empire style in France that followed were to become the three pillars, though different, on which Biedermeier furniture designs were based.

The French Empire style

A decisive change took place, again this time in France. Ignited by the French Revolution and furthered by the influence of the middle class Directory government, the Empire style began to develop in the mid-seventeen nineties. Its spread, though, was directly linked with the name of Napoleon, who had himself proclaimed First Consul of the French Republic in 1799. Architecture and interior decoration now appeared in the style of the Roman emperors, as requested by Napoleon, and as propagated by the artists Prud'hon and David and translated by the architects Percier and Fontaine.

The German Empire style

The more and more prevalent pattern drawings, theoretical writings, and journals, as well as the exports of renowned furniture makers such as Jacob Desmalter, paved the way in Germany for the growth of this monumental style that strove for greatness and power. The Empire style developed first in the regions occupied by Napoleon or ruled by his relatives and the sympathetic principalities that were brought together in the Confederation of the Rhine in 1806.

The Empire style furniture that still exists at the Residence in Ludwigsburg or Wilhelmshöhe Castle in Kassel lets us sense the attraction of the heavy forms of the early seventeen seventies. It shows a further development with the blending of various geometrical figures and inclusion of the antique Greco-Roman and Egyptian forms, and make clear Germany's own strivings within the standard forms of the French style.

The lightness and grace of the harmonious Queue style seems to have been forgotten. Furniture, whether for containing or sitting, rests on weighty, immovable bases like monuments or thrones, held fast to the floor, as it were, by powerful paw-like feet. The surfaces of the bodies are compelling. Right-angle bends disappear in favor of smooth and horizontal friezes. The tension of internal opposites makes the furniture come alive. For example, large smooth surfaces contrast with slim frames and *vice versa*, or thin top plates lie on weighty bodies. Pilasters, caryatids and columns, griffins, lions and sphinxes, formerly used as accentuating surface decorations, became independent, load bearing members of the construction in the Empire style, as can be recognized especially clearly in tables.

The preferred wood, mahogany, with its unified, compact-looking surfaces, was livened up by added bronze ornaments whose artistic formation and technical production were brilliant. Military emblems of Imperial Rome clarify their imperial character. Mythological scenes of ancient Greece, symbols of the Egyptian pharaohs and heraldic devices were scattered about the surfaces, often indiscriminately, paired with palmettoes, acanthus leaves, or staffs of pearls and eggs. They completely overwhelm the inlay decor.

Thus furniture was created without visible influence of a cabinet-maker, apparently designed by architects, monuments that really bordered on the monumental and could just as well have been hammered out of marble or cast in bronze. But it is also furniture whose dominating fascination the furniture student cannot turn his back on.

For this style that was intended strictly to make an impression with its imperial name, dictatorially steered to the reawakening of long-dead cultures and thus ruling out its own initiative and imagination, the political fact of Napoleon's fall from power was enough to bring it to an abrupt end — although many a German residence, so far away from the focal point of Paris, still clung to it until the beginning of Historicism. The successful "Wars of Liberation" against Napoleon, linked with so much hope for political and social changes, also oppressed the Empire style in Germany to a great extent; but as Georg Himmelheber points out, without forming a truly German variant.

The Austrian Empire style

The situation in Austria was very different. In its capital of Vienna, some distance away from France both geographically and politically, a genuine, independent development of Empire style came about. Here there was not as much agitation for a prescribed French repertoire of forms as, for example, in southern Germany, but instead a gentle reshaping as an expression of a tendency toward comfort, involving the established forms of the harmonious Queue style, which characterized the Empire period in Austria — meaning in Vienna.

Even though the Austrian imperial court cannot be regarded, as the German residences can, as a direct promoter of the Empire style, still it was required by law that only those who had been trained in drawing for a prescribed length of time at the Vienna Academy of Formative Arts were allowed to take the master's test. And in 1807, Emperor Franz I had an "Imperial and Royal Factory Production Cabinet" established, where Austrian-made objects of commercial art were put on display. This was a fruitful foundation in terms of both art and handicraft; on the one hand, it allowed creative designing of the artisan; on the other, it made these new products accessible to greater masses of people.

The numerous design drawings and objects of interior decoration that resulted show a well-defined difference from the French style. In Vienna there is lighter furniture, intended for domestic and private life. Cut-off corners with columns and an airy substructure took away the severe, space-consuming effect of the cube. New forms of furniture were developed from the oval and the lyre shape, either thoroughly developed into a whole piece or added as a design element. Naturally, for case pieces and tables, the designs were oriented to the monumental spirit of French Empire times, but one can almost always find in the Viennese interpretation a transposition into a more sentimental, playful style.

For heraldic emblems, stiffened sphinxes, griffins and lions were replaced by swans, caryatids and antique-style figure elements in positions of motion; and no longer were they cast in bronze, but rather enlivened by the warm tones of gilded wood. The bronze hardware that was used without a claim to being Imperial utilized horns of plenty, vases, garlands and scenes from Greek mythology applied sparingly for accent. What remained dominant was the use of mahogany veneer as a contrast to the gilded bronzes, rarely livened up with inlaid ornamental bands or painted inlays.

Furniture for sitting regained its lightness, already achieved in the Queue style, from airily pierced backs. Through rounded, curved or rolled shapes flowing into and blending with each other, chairs and sofas stand once again on lighter, conical legs that are often curved. This organic form in the Viennese Empire style must be regarded as a direct forerunner, in interior decoration, of the middle class Biedermeier style.

Biedermeier style Development and Characteristics

The starting point for this discussion must be the year 1815, which is generally regarded as the beginning of the Biedermeier era. With the victory of the Coalition armies over the empire of Napoleon in France, the Empire style also lost its power, and the strivings of the Congress of Vienna for a new order in Europe at first encouraged hope for a different political and social outlook. The presumed victory of the middle class over the rights of the aristocracy, the guarantees of constitutions and freedom of the press, the concept of a free form of government introduced chiefly by the younger generation, all had results that did not leave out the handicrafts.

With the introduction of commercial freedom and the trade organizations that developed from it, the regular trade fairs, the public display of models and trade journals in libraries or reading circles came the broad-based need for education and technical knowledge. With this new incentive, which was the foundation of the Biedermeier era, and the increased self-awareness of the artisan who was born in a time of economic depression, the Empire style could no longer serve as a model. The imperial overtones of the Empire style were contrary to the new concepts of freedom, and a lavish interior decor showed itself to be too expensive for the economically weaker middle class.

Attributed to Franz Krüger, self-portrait of the artist with the Göbel couple.

When the Continental blockade against British products, imposed by Napoleon in 1806, was broken, a vigorous increase in trade activity resulted. In many ways, Britain could serve as a model for the new era since modern machines and tools were already in use there. Thus, a quick economic and industrial development was possible. But the British arts of handicrafts and fashions, oriented as they were to middle class life, also found widespread acceptance in Germany. Not only were up-to-date designs drawn, but English furniture styles of the late eighteenth century (as already discussed in the "Origin" chapter) influenced new German furniture designs with their newly gained functionality and fidelity to material. It was above all else Thomas Sheridan's pattern book that served as an example for this new orientation. In this respect, there are parallels with the influence of the British interior art on the Louis XVI style, whose "domestic" forms in turn are very similar to those of Biedermeier furniture. It was not the mighty, white-and-gold-ornamented forms of the early seventeen seventies that were used as models by the German Biedermeier furniture makers, but the light and decorative pieces of the harmonious Queue style that were turned to now. The results can be seen most clearly in the lightness of the chairs with their conical legs, pierced backs and increased openness of design.

The art of Biedermeier furniture should not be regarded as a toned-down, late form of Empire, as can be read in numerous publications. Naturally, as the last of the three Classic styles, Biedermeier was oriented toward the Empire style, its immediate predecessor, and grew out of it, developing contemporary forms and utilizing its ornamentation. But also Biedermeier was a direct reaction to the Empire style and was based above all on rejection of the political, social and spiritual conditions of the Empire. Out of this rejection, Biedermeier developed with its own individual style of furniture.

An essential difference between Biedermeier and Empire styles is shown in the "theoretical" origin of Biedermeier furniture. No longer did the architect or artist make the design, but rather the cabinetmaker himself, trained in the drawing schools of the now-numerous German polytechnic organizations, gave the model its form. Forms and decorations were, of course, taken from the well-known pattern drawings, but when they were actually made they were ultimately based on the individual builder's own creative imagination and knowledge of the needs and background of the job itself.

In terms of technology, of course, there were many innovations in tools and machines available to the German cabinetmakers after 1815, such as the padsaw, better planes and planing machines, saws, drills, slitters and veneer cutters; but it was important at that time that not too many of them found their way into the workshops. In that time of multi-layered social changes, one stuck to the old traditions.

The increase in imports, the great competition resulting from the lifting of guild control, and the economic depression during the war years surely were not conducive to this development either. Technical versatility, though — in comparison with the Historicism style — was not at all necessary, since the middle class customers did not demand it. J. A. Lux remarked on this subject as early as 1902: "It is noteworthy that all the furniture is purely the product of carpenters, and the only and natural decoration was found in the neat and solid workmanship."

The lack of ornamentation is one of the outstanding, and unfortunately often misunderstood, qualities of Biedermeier furniture, which will be discussed in brief below and explained in greater detail in the chapter on furniture design.

The three goals for designers insisted on again and again, particularly in Art Nouveau or Bauhaus style and also stressed today, those of *fidelity*, *functionality* and *mobility*, were cautiously advanced for the first time in Biedermeier furniture. *Fidelity*, understood as visual development of the style out of the material (wood), includes the constant reduction of surfaces, architectonic elements, rails, backs, etc. on the drawing board. This goal is clearly recognizable in the design and thus is achievable in its creative origin. *Functionality* requires a different point of view, though it is a part of every furniture style, yet in different forms of expression. The furniture users almost always valued the criterion of a good impression more highly than that of purposeful living. In Biedermeier, though, a remarkably great compromise in favor of livability was desired, as we can see by looking, for example, at a table from that era. The Biedermeier table is usually round, standing on a central pillar and thus offering easy access all around without deep frames or equally disturbing legs and obtrusive feet at the corners. *Mobility* is clearly demonstrated in Biedermeier chairs with their pierced backs, or in case or writing furniture with their balanced proportions. The many small functional pieces of furniture remain variable by nature and thus express the character of movability and exchangeability.

Unfortunately, it is a widespread bad habit — especially in the art business — to characterize Biedermeier furniture from the first fifteen years, because of time-related values, as "late Empire". This error is abetted by the appearance of columns, caryatids, cat's-feet, and elements of Classic architecture or corresponding bronze hardware. This probably happens often too in failing to recognize the fact that, in the Biedermeier furniture art, the style was indebted to Classicism, though with clearly limited, sytle-creating characteristics.

The Empire furniture was intended to be a purely architectural form and thus makes a completely different impression from the Biedermeier furniture created by a cabinetmaker. In Empire furniture, we find various cubes, set in front of or on top of each other, blended into each other or lined up next to each other, often varied with convex or concave shapes. In Biedermeier furniture, pillars have neither an architectural nor a space-dividing function in the sense of Classical arrangement. Just like the caryatids and other decorative elements, they must subordinate themselves to the flat surfaces, which results in a certain arrangement of the frontal appearance. This appearance constitutes another typical characteristic of the furniture of that time.

The appearance of frame-filling design is avoided when possible in Biedermeier style, for it would only impinge on the flat surfaces. When frame-filling designs appear, their effect is weakened by the unified covering of the veneer, running the long way, blending in the sides and centered around a middle axis [symmetrical], also emphasizing the flatness of the surface. Any other elements used, such as friezes, recessed patterns in the form of geometric figures such as circle segments, rhombuses or rectangles, are subordinated to this uniform "outer surface" effect.

One also encounters curved shapes in Biedermeier furniture. They differ, of course, from the flowing curves of Baroque or Rococo, for they are usually limited to table and chair legs, the back of a chair, or furniture parts like bases, shelves or crowns. But whole pieces too, especially small pieces, are shaped in spherical form and show the talent of the artisan.

The decorative elements of Biedermeier are those of Classicism, but they are subordinated to the flat surfaces, and bronze is often replaced by gilded wood. Also three-dimensional applied details made of molded sawdust and other "mixed materials" were used; applied horns of plenty, dolphins or swans can be found in the arms of sofas or the frames of tables. Animal feet are also still in use for case furniture or table legs, but one can see the same change in all of them: they look less naturalistic, but instead often appear stylized, and at the same time they are portrayed more tenderly. Therefore they correspond to that transposition that the Austrian Empire style had already completed. The pierced chair backs, as they did in Queue style, offer many possibilities for decoration. The lyre shape enjoyed great popularity; it served as a decorative ornament, was included in the design as a support or side piece of tables, in fact it defined whole types of furniture, even though it was often stylized and barely recognizable. Bronze hardware did not appear, as in the Empire style, as decorations on flat surfaces, but was only used sparingly and purposefully for handles or lock shields. Most of the time, stamped sheet brass was used for handles and lock shields and for these there were few actual motifs; for the most part, they were adopted from Queue or Empire style. Sometimes these metal parts disappear altogether, and inset coat-of-arms or diamond-shaped lock shields in ebonized wood or bone appear instead.

There should be as little distraction as possible from the natural beauty and carefully selected structure of the wood for they give the Biedermeier furniture its calm, homey atmosphere. The lively grain patterns of the wood often served as the only decoration, but value was also given to bright, warm-toned woods that achieved the desired homey atmosphere. The wood of fruit trees combines both characteristics in splendid fashion: walnut and cherry wood in particular, glued to the body as veneers, were second only to mahogany as the most important woods utilized during this time. Economic factors surely must have played a major role in the preference for native woods, for mahogany, used almost exclusively in the Empire style, had to be imported and was expensive. Nevertheless, mahogany was often used for furniture made in the south as well as more often and more traditionally in the north of Germany, and in northern and central Germany ash, birch and elm wood also were popular. Oak was used extremely rarely, since its surface is unsuitable for taking a polish.

Maple wood, light in color and radiating coolness, was used mainly for inlays. These inlays were not as marquetry panels, but rather as sparce accents such as folded stars, tendrils, blossoms, umbrella or shell motifs. Ribbonlike frames and inlays never hold the entire form together, but rather contour the individual cubes. Only in the construction of, for example, a part of a secretary is one aware of the creative challenge the inlay presents. Woods of various colors, tricks of perspective, masonry, diamond and cube patterns as well as small architectonic details can be found inside secretaries but usually are not visible when the writing panel is closed. Paintings and transfer decorations applied directly to the wood can also be found occasionally.

Now, at the end of this discussion, it may be permissable to quote J. A. Lux again: "One is quickly ready to state that those times possessed no art. One completely overlooks the fact that the creativity that, to be sure, did not produce any monumental art at that time, was devoted all the more intensively to the very important small work in all areas of formation, and provided the appearance, almost extinct today, of a general personal and ethnic culture."

Curt Wilhelm Gropius, **Living room in the house of Theater Director C. W. Gropius,** *watercolor, circa 1830, 30.8 x 30.5 cm. Markish Museum, Berlin.*

Lands and Localities

In the eighteenth century, the decisive artistic influences came above all from the royal courts and residences. Their impact on furniture building, as on other arts, created styles in certain centers and regions. The courtly model, the firmly encoded guild regulations and toll barriers caused furniture to be made in these times that, by analysis of their styles, can lead us more or less precisely to their areas of origin. But these circumstances all lost their influence at the beginning of the Biedermeier era. For the first time we are now dealing with a style that developed out of the middle class atmosphere. In the developing industrialization that came with Historicism, clues as to the origins of a particular piece of furniture disappeared almost completely. Therefore it is often difficult to determine or even suggest local characteristics in Biedermeier furniture, and it requires a different sort of observation. Attributing or suggesting certain masters, regions and centers, for home furnishings of the "Vormärz" era, as with art objects in general, can be undertaken only with the greatest caution and care, although local elements of style certainly did come into being.

Biedermeier style in Vienna

The Habsburg monarchy with its metropolis of Vienna, focal point of Europe in 1815 thanks to the Congress of Vienna there, was also the center and focal point of the Biedermeier age in a social sense. From Vienna, where a materially secure and well-to-do middle class possessed the self-assurance for a culture-bearing leadership role, the most fruitful ideas radiated. After the ultimate rejection of French hegemony, Vienna was a center of spirit and culture in Europe in many ways and was strong enough to fuse the most varied influences into its own synthesis.

In the Empire period, the Viennese furniture makers had already developed a characteristic style (see page 17). Its more popular and imaginative forms differ clearly from those of both the French style and its German derivatives. Developing from this native and secure understanding of form, Viennese Biedermeier furniture can be understood, more than the furniture from anywhere else, as a direct, organic outgrowth of the Empire style, and it is characterized by particularly noteworthy, artistically mature products of high quality. The preference in Vienna for unconventional, spirited forms can be recognized in the lyre secretaries known since the Empire times. In them the lyre, a detail that, until then, had been added as a decorative element, came to define the entire outline of a piece of furniture. A further example is the scroll. It appears on chiffonieres, commodes and night tables as a form-defining body, as well as being used for the arms of sofas or the feet of tables, whereby the lower roll is formed like a cylinder and serves as a base. The changing role of various geometrical forms, standing in a row or extending into each other, dominates Viennese Biedermeier furniture just as surely: circles, ovals, cylinders, rectangles or trapezoids appear in harmony with pillars, posts, arched elements and harmoniously drawn-in plaques.

The admiration for rounded surfaces reached its high point in those masterpieces of the artisan's craft, the hemispherical sewing tables and the completely round globe tables. Although the cabinetmaker George Remmington had already obtained a patent for a comparable writing desk in Britain in 1806, these jewels of Biedermeier furniture art were developed to the fullest by the Viennese ebony workers and rank, in terms of their brilliance in handiwork and technique, among the most beautiful and highest-quality products that we know from this era.

To what a great extent the Viennese products were imbued with the imagination of their designers, most of whom were also their builders, is demonstrated by the variety of the pieces still in existence: patent secretaries, ladies' writing tables, pillar commodes, reading and writing stands, work, sewing, toilette and flower tables, card tables, etagères, servantes, cuspidors, stove screens and many others. Like the Empire furniture, this furniture was often made of mahogany, but native woods with a lively grain pattern — like walnut, cherry and ash — were also used willingly.

For inlays used ornamentally yet sparingly and deliberately to highlight a particular surface, the light colored but unfigured maple wood was usually used. Decorative elements could also be painted dircetly onto the wood. Like the bronze hardware that was used almost unchanged from the Empire style, the decorative elements were not placed stiffly, but rather were scattered apparently at random, subordinated to the surface. This scattered placement was also true for applied figural decorations made of gilded wood or other materials which glitter — in contrast to the cold bronze of the Empire style — and radiate a similarly tangible warmth. In and of themselves, the ornaments do not achieve any compelling expression in a sophisticated sense, but rather appear tender, playful, and sometimes even jolly.

Vienna, the metropolis that led the way, placed the furniture makers located there in the advantageous position of working not only for the comfort-seeking and well-to-do middle class of the city, but at the same time of being able to supply the extensive outlying areas. The export of their popular furniture also provided these artisans with a solid foundation. In 1816, there were 875 independent master carpenters in Vienna; in 1823, already 951. The majority of them were directly subordinate to the court in the practice of their craft and thus free from any guild domination. Some of them ran actual factories.

Probably the best-known and most important Viennese master carpenter of the time was Josef Danhauser, who employed over 100 workers as early as 1808. In his store, *Etablissement für alle Gegenstände des Ameublements*, founded in 1804, he sold not only the furniture made in his factory, but also a wide variety of general housewares such as drapes, carpets, clocks and even glassware. The Austrian Museum of Applied Art possesses more than 2500 of Danhauser's design drawings. They provide an inclusive overview of the breadth and type of his production and his apparently never-ending imagination that resulted in new forms

Viennese scene by *L. C. Hoffmeister, pictorial clock with three scenes, oil on metal, signed and dated "Wien 1826", 57 x 82 cm.*

and decorations. But Danhauser also supplied designs that come alive through straight lines and static calm which, reduced to the constructive, have their effect without any decoration.

The fact that furniture made in this significant center of production can be identified clearly, on the basis of the preserved drawings, is rare. These pages illustrate another important fact that distinguishes the Viennese masters of that time: all of them were experienced designers, for only those who had been trained in drawing for a presecirbed length of time were allowed to take the master's test. In private drawing schools, a typical example of which was that of Prussian-born Karl Schmidt, carpenters, as well as other artisans, could be instructed and thus did not have to depend on the design drawings of outsiders.

In contrast to its political position, the government was very interested in the further development of artisans and technicians in terms of the new spirit of the times. Thus in 1815, a polytechnical school was established, which later took over the contents of the Product Cabinet, and put domestic products on display in comparative competitions. This attitude gave Viennese furniture builders a secure, solid trade, which is reflected in those lovable, imaginative home furnishings which were made to the highest quality.

South Germany

The fortunate prerequisite conditions in Vienna are seen in comparable strength nowhere else in the German world. In Munich, probably the most important center of southern Germany, there were, for example, only 44 independent furniture masters in 1822. Munich was a small, rural city at that time, and its court, particularly under Ludwig I, followed Classical styles. The active construction work carried out under Ludwig I also resulted in a comparably elegant style of interior decoration. The influential architects Friedrich von Gärtner and Leo von Klenze (the latter also active in the field of interior decorating) both worked in the Classical style of the court and had nothing to do with the middle class Biedermeier trend. Instead, they got involved surprisingly early with historical trends, or else they simply followed the Empire style that predominated in court circles. This officially prescribed style trend left the middle class few possibilities for development. The handicrafts were left to private initiative, for they received no decisive promotion from the court.

Businessman Karl Zeller took the first step, so important to the handicraft, by founding a private polytechnical organization in 1816. In earlier years, he had published magazines and journals that highlighted inventions and innovations as well as the problems of buying and selling, and also organized exhibitions in a hotel.

The few identified pieces from these early times are simple yet noble furniture, often still bound to the Empire style in terms of their proportions. The base and flat surface still had to subordinate themselves to the strict flatness so often found and are completely contained in a clear outline which may be featured by inlaid or painted-on ornamental bands. As a further characteristic, we can observe copperplate prints that were applied directly to the wood by a transfer process and may adorn not only the outside but also the inside surfaces. This transfer process of decoration, better known in the field of ceramics, was used by Johann Georg Hiltl, who first exhibited furinture decorated in this way at the fair of art and commercial art objects in 1818.

In the other South German cities that had renowned names in furniture building in the eighteenth century, Biedermeier furniture of high quality was also produced. Augsburg, Nuremberg, Regensburg, Bamberg, Bayreuth, Würzburg and Ansbach must be noted as important centers.

A similar situation to that in Bavaria and Munich existed in the other two south German states of Baden and Württemberg. In Karlsruhe, Friedrich Weinbrenner, and in Stuttgart and Ludwigsburg Nikolaus Friedrich Thouret, used their antique-oriented tastes during the Empire period to set definite accents in stately, court-influenced furniture, and these trends were to develop further in the times that followed.

Mainz

The focal point for Biedermeier furniture of the southwest German area was Mainz. In the eighteenth century, craftsmen in Mainz produced the splendid Baroque furniture that must be ranked among the loveliest furniture art in Germany. A progressive guild here promoted its work well into the nineteenth century and even up to the twentieth. Johann Wolfgang Kussmann, Wilhelm Kimbel, Philipp Anton Bambé and their furniture workshops and factories represented a great tradition of craftsmanship that also characterized Mainz in the nineteenth century as an important center in the production of Biedermeier furniture. In the year 1816, more than 180 independent masters were active there, and without guild pressure they enjoyed professional freedom and found favorable conditions for healthy competition.

As a result of this flourishing craftsmanship, the export of furniture increased as did contact with masters and workshops in the nearby regions. The entire Southwest was oriented to products from Mainz. For case furniture, the simple box form with clear cubic shape reduced to the essentials dominated. A flat surface and optical unity resulted from the use of lively mottled wood characteristic of this area; the wood covered angles, projections and depressions evenly and thus subordinated them to the total design.

Applied, flanking columns, often painted black, served as the only decoration of the wood other than its natural beauty. But the builders were also well-versed in the production of those charming, imaginative small pieces that were not just the domain of the Viennese cabinetmakers, but were also produced by Mainz craftsmen. It may be no coincidence that Wilhelm Kimbel was traveling in Vienna before he opened his own shop in Mainz in 1815. Fine inlaid or painted-on bands of tendrils are found on projections, friezes and stripes on case furniture as well as on the backs of chairs. The chair backs utilized the bowed form, and the added decoration was typically a transparent, clearly recognizable ornament.

The favorite woods in southern and southwestern Germany were the warm-toned cherry and walnut traditional in the region. Mahogany, birch and maple enjoyed a certain popularity but were used less frequently.

The Rhineland and lower Rhine area cabinetmakers were influenced by the work from Mainz. The carved oak furniture that was once so treasured here disappeared completely, for the whole scope of production was devoted to modern veneered furniture. Only now and then did carved components appear, perhaps on the arms of chairs and sofas or on table legs. Dolphins, whose amusing portrayal was also taken over from the South, as well as horns of plenty or foliage were preferred. North German style influences can also be seen in this furniture, but they are found in details rather than in the defining overall form.

North Germany

In northern Germany, with its free Hanseatic cities, the Biedermeier style developed by different routes than in the South. Since the Hanseatic cities were already set up as middle class communities in the eighteenth century, the Empire style was never really able to spread or establish itself there, not even during the French occupation of 1810-1813. Therefore the Biedermeier style here did not originate as a reaction to the upper class court style. Rather, it developed directly from the Queue style that had been cultivated by the middle class of northern Germany. The Queue style had evolved from British influences and enjoying great popularity in northern Germany until the emergence of Biedermeier. Thus there was not a return to the Queue style as in the South, but instead an almost direct stylistic evolution, into which, in the end, the heavier forms of Empire style also flowed.

But the choice of wood was different in the north than in the south. The close trade relationship with Britain enabled problem-free importing of mahogany, which became the preferred wood of the North German cabinetmakers. Birch, which can be found as a mottled or knotty wood, was also used. Cherry and walnut, on the other hand, were only used now and then. Case furniture experienced cube-like development, as elsewhere, but also tended to be shaped with upward extensions. For example, Biedermeier writing desks from northern Germany often bear an architectural addition above their actual body where several flat plates are placed one above the other in stepped form, leading the glance inexorably upward. Such stepped designs also appear in cabinets and showcases, and such, in connection with gable designs or crowns on pedestals. Superstructures and additions in the most varied geometric forms, which either formed rows or blended into each other, were popular. The play of changing forms is also found in decorative shapes set into flat surfaces, such as gate arches, circles, squares, rectangles or rhombuses. As accents, the shapes can spread over two drawers, come out in contrasting light and dark shades, or support bronze hardware or painting. A further characteristic of northern German Biedermeier style is the use of stepped, overlapping bureau drawers which are sometimes built in arched form. The essential characteristics of Biedermeier furniture — unity of appearance, formation from the nature of the wood, and striving for flatness — are also those of this furniture. And in northern German furniture a panel often stretches between the feet, shelflike, closing off the open pedestal area.

The British influence, especially in furniture for sitting, is apparent in the restrained elegance of the designs as well as the frequent use of shell ornaments. Tables with folding panels or side pieces also developed from British models, as did the wide variety of utilitarian small furniture with which the middle class, always thinking of domesticity and livability, liked to surround itself. Since so much furniture of this kind was made, one must recognize the widespread emphasis on the quality of life in northern Germany in the Biedermeier era as well as the cabinetmaking ability and artistic imagination of the furniture makers.

Berlin

The capital city and center of a state (Prussia) of considerable size, Berlin was the site of vigorous building activity in the years of the Biedermeier era. Architect Karl Friedrich Schinkel was contracted to furnish plans for city buildings as well as their interior decor. Like those of Leo von Klenze who was similarly employed in Munich, Schinkel's structures show elements of Classicism and Historicism. For the court, he also created impressive furniture in late Empire style. But unlike Klenze, Schinkel used Biedermeier elements in both architecture and furniture design. His ultimate mastery of both is seen in the Academy of Architecture which was built under his direction, and in the very detailed design drawings created by him for furniture construction. The court cabinetmakers Johann Christian Sewening and Karl Georg Wandschaff made numerous pieces of furniture from his designs. Schinkel was also interested in making his design drawings available to other artisans — and in Berlin in 1816, over 1300 masters and journeymen were registered. This goal became feasible after 1821 when he, along with the state councillor Peter Wilhelm Christian Beuth, published these drawings in the journal *Vorbilder für Fabrikanten und Handwerker*.

Characteristic of Schinkel's designs is an elegant facade of the furniture. His increased use of columns, architraves and other architectural elements, including facade details of historical buildings and antique style ornamentation, very rich for the Biedermeier time, were undoubtedly inspired by the Empire style. In spite of this, his overall conception and smooth construction of the parts clearly shows that this furniture belongs to the Biedermeier. There are no elements that dominate the design. It is not an architect's or artist's theoretical academy style that forces the form and composition on the furniture, but rather a craftsman's mastery of the material (wood) that was securely dominated by Schinkel.

Schinkel's striking designs, created for the court and nobility, could be modified by an artisan to suit the wishes of his customer. The cabinetmakers could just as well turn back to simpler designs if they did not comprehend his designs. Many possibilities existed for them in the artisans' organizations and private polytechnical societies that existed then.

The styles of furniture and decoration of the North German area were also appreciated in Berlin and Prussia. The use of a strongly formed front facade and rich use of ornamental elements may be clues about the origin of some pieces. Mahogany and birch were used often followed by cherry, walnut and ash. As for the craftsmanship quality of the Berlin products, the patented secretary of Adolph Friedrich Voigt at the Museum of Commercial Art in Berlin-Köpenick can be regarded as typical. This striking secretary fulfills, in impressive style, the striving for functionalism and mobility that characterize Biedermeier and also demonstrates that its builder clearly based his design on a pattern in British designer Thomas Sheraton's *Drawing Book*.

Central Germany

In central Germany, Brunswick, Dresden and Erfurt were eighteenth-century furniture centers known beyond their own areas; their products were of high quality and had their own style. The inspiring power that radiated from these centers into nearby regions — unlike that of Mainz and the Southwest — was no longer noticeable in the Biedermeier era. The central German furniture style supported by the middle class was a mixture that employed elements of two different styles. Settled between the North and the South, the area produced furniture that reflects the two style influences equally. The fact that the furniture with these outside influences does not have to have an unpleasant combination verifies the middle class, folk character of Biedermeier furniture.

Brunswick Biedermeier furniture clearly shows the influence of Berlin. The designs published so well by Franz-Josef Christiani and preserved in the city archives and city museum there underscore this fact. They join other Westphalian products such as, for example, those of Hannover, in subordinating themselves to the North German sense of style in their overall conception. But a great deal was known in Brunswick about the use of South German influences as well.

In Hesse, on the other hand, furniture making was oriented more to the artistically strong South, particularly since the Elector of Hesse had employed the Classicist Christoph Jussow (active under King Jerome Bonaparte) to provide designs in the late Empire style.

Influences from Berlin are just as provable in Thuringia and Saxony as those from the South, and the more playful styles of Vienna are clearly recognizable there too. As early as 1816, after all, there was an exhibition of Austrian products held in Leipzig; and in Bohemia — thus completing the circle we have made around the German culture area — the Viennese style was followed to a great extent.

In summary, however, among the great volume of preserved Biedermeier furniture, it is still difficult to ascribe a piece to a particular region. The middle class essence of this style, the broad opportunities for the artisan, and a balance of form and decoration combined to create this popular, comparatively simple furniture for the Biedermeier style of living.

13. Writing Secretary *"On August 6, 1824 Friedrich Heinrich Eduard Müller presented this design for his masterpiece." Braunschweig City Archives, Braunschweig City Museum (photo).*

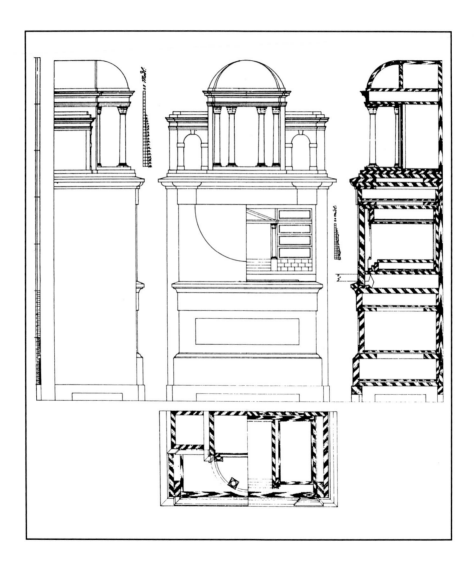

Limits and Late Forms

In general terms, the year of 1815 is regarded as the beginning of the Biedermeier era. It is the year in which the end of the preceding Napoleonic Age was affirmed by the Congress of Vienna. According to the will of the people, who had fought in the Wars of Liberation with such great hopes, though, it was also supposed to be the end of absolute monarchy, oppression and *noblesse oblige*. Inspired by thoughts of freedom that affected their political and social life equally, a hopeful middle class, believing in the future, grew stronger and wanted to make its own dreams come true in the arts as well as in commerce. In this fruitful time, a purely middle class, down-to-earth and personal style could develop — the Biedermeier style.

The aristocracy, however, in positions of authority now as before (since their power structure was reimposed by the Karlsbad Decrees of 1819), soon realized that this development would also put their class in a questionable position. Their reaction was persecution of every sign of free thinking, censorship, and espionage; and therefore life in general became concentrated in the private sector on home and family. The people's withdrawal into private life led to a noticeable middle class living style. In the end, the creation of a small, pleasant, cloistered world made identification with the middle class's ideals successful, or at least helped them to forget their anxiety and insecurity. For the furniture building of the time, this meant that, not the least because of the social and economic conditions, no showy furniture was promoted; instead, the majority of the people wanted simple, livable pieces.

Late Biedermeier Style After 1830

Until around 1830, Biedermeier furniture can be understood to be a pure interpretation of style bound to Classicism. Then it lost its extensive influential character. For Biedermeier furniture, 1830 marks a time of change, but this is certainly not to be regarded as its disappearance. Just as every great style has its evolution and is changed by interpretations across the map, so the Biedermeier style had a late form which lasted until after 1840.

The Biedermeier style enjoyed a certain popularity in the private sector of court life even though fancy and public rooms were furnished, as before, in Empire style, as we have seen already in the examples in Munich and Berlin. From 1830 on, though, the Napoleonic style in its less elegant late form often found its way into the middle class living culture. Along with it, there appeared more designs that showed an increasing inclusion of historical elements. The exhibitions, fairs, publications and pattern books, which became more numerous at that time, function as a barometer of the prevailing style.

Astonishingly, in the German-speaking area in the last years of the eighteenth century, a few individual furniture designs already featured elements of Gothic style. Along with the "Old French Taste", meaning the Baroque style that was also found at times, the Gothic elements were reserved exclusively for the royal courts.

Biedermeier furniture of the early phase (1815-1830) only shows Gothic tracery now and then. Not until the last third of the nineteenth century were the revived styles (Gothic, Baroque, and later Renaissance, Rococo and other foreign style trends) featured in furniture design to their full extent, finally culminating in Historicism. For cabinetmakers who had followed the Biedermeier style, this "new style" tendency meant transplanting long-antiquated decorations into fashionable furniture. Only around 1850 did late Biedermeier style lose its status, along with the late Empire style that ran parallel with it.

It is not a change in the basic form that identifies the late phase of Biedermeier furniture but the details and how they are used: now rounded and even ribbed angles appeared. They direct the eye to the sides, just as does the decorative profile that runs around three sides or the waved and knobbed frieze that cuts through and divides the flat surfaces. Along with the double scrolls that are often used as closings, these details result in a certain dissolution of the forms that was clearly defined in the past. The supporting architectural elements, which can be regarded as carry-overs from the Empire style, are included more emphatically. Now they no longer appear purely playful and therefore dispensable, but rather they form a vital component of the designs.

The arch, previously a tense, feathering curve, now dissolves and softens into flowing lines. The base, feet, legs, back, arms, bars or panels form a richly decorated silhouetted shape. The central columns of tables are made much stronger after 1830, and also appear less sharply defined. In general, shapes turned on a lathe appear increasingly more often, as seen in the front legs of North German chairs. The s-shaped cornice trim, unknown in the earlier phase, is often added to top rails or cabinet fronts after 1830.

Another important identifying mark of the late period is the enrichment of decorative motifs. On the one hand, flat inlays of all kinds, showing flowers, tendrils, leaves or other historic decorations, are very popular. On the other hand, the use of high-relief, three-dimensional or sculpted applied decorations also increases. Leaves, swans, eagles, horns of plenty and fans are inset for decoration and can even dominate whole sections of the furniture.

Cabinet makers Wilhelm Kimbel from Mainz and Johann Nepomuk Geyer from Innsbruck and their workshops are two outstanding makers of furniture in the late Biedermeier style. Their furniture typifies the use of earlier forms with the inclusion of later style features.

Only Historicism style and the industrialization linked with it brought on the end of the Biedermeier style. By the middle of the nineteenth century, these influences began to work their all-inclusive consequences. Even so, Michael Thonet of Boppard on the Rhine had, in the mid-eighteen thirties, begun to develop mass production of his bentwood furniture with interchangeable parts. He achieved world fame for his innovations only after his move to Vienna in 1842.

Only around 1900, after the Biedermeier style had been scorned and ridiculed for more than half a century, were the first attempts to re-evaluate the style made. In 1896, the Austrian Museum of Art and Industry in Vienna prepared a major exhibition on the Congress of Vienna. Observations on the history of art followed, often still designating Biedermeier as a derivitive of the Empire style. But more and more, the independent nature of Biedermeier style became recognized and its furniture was also re-evaluated. Furniture design was seen to have developed (like Art Nouveau from the reaction to the pluralism of styles and variety of forms of Historicism) from the "antique virtues" of Empire and Biedermeier equally. At the exhibitions, furnishings of whole rooms in Biedermeier style were shown. On the one hand, this was furniture that had been copied faithfully from historical patterns; on the other, it had been reinvented in modified form. For functional use and fidelity to material, both definite characteristics of Biedermeier, were recognized and valued anew around 1900. They gave the decisive impetus to twentieth-century furniture building and eventually found their realization in the splendid style of the Bauhaus.

The Furniture

Room Interiors

At the time of the Congress of Vienna (1815), the public building style was that of early Classicism. The modest middle class home and apartment house could not tear themselves away from this style. Only gradually did residences become small geometric shapes with balanced proportions. In architecture as well as furniture, the emphasis changed from outside splendor to inside comfort, conforming completely to the nature of Biedermeier.

Interiors of the time are shown to us in paintings, water-colors and, above all, the copperplate engravings so thoroughly popular at the time. As their central feature, they often show the patriarchal family in the midst of an almost modest and yet lovely home scene or a social occasion with music, games or reading. It is not the fine, lavish salon that is the place of this gathering. It is the "good room", furnished as if by chance, whose lighthearted use of space illustrates life style and living culture as one indivisible, self-defining unity. The furniture, in terms of shape and size, fit the prescribed spatial conditions as well as human proportions. A symmetrical arrangement can only be found where it happened all by itself. For the first time, one encounters a widespread, unforced style of interior decor designed to meet individual needs, with the resident family forming its focal point. It was not the courtly-academic art of interior decor forcing their living culture on people from outside; instead, it developed organically, completely by itself, from the wish for coziness and happiness. The need for harmony between man and environment at that time caused furniture to be made to reflect this symbiotic relationship; furniture that, in its simplicity and comfort, radiates the feeling of being at home, and therefore has become so desirable.

The dwelling rooms were painted in light colors or whitewashed; only the well-to-do middle class adorned their walls with striped wallpaper, usually ornamented with small floral designs. An ornamental frieze often set off the walls from the ceiling, which was often decorated with rosettes. From the center of the ceiling, glass chandeliers, ceiling crowns made of wood and other materials, or simple petroleum lamps hung down. The floor was made of planed planks or boards; it was seldom parqueted. Gathered curtains bathed the rooms in a gentle light.

Furniture Types

The **secretary** occupied a certain place in the living room. It was not so often the upright secretary with folding front panel, well known since Baroque times, but rather the writing cabinet with smaller proportions and a smooth front. The traditional design had three drawers in the bottom, and over them the big folding writing panel and, to finish the design, a built-in top drawer. Above the opening panel there often also arose a cabinet with one door architecturally formed. The inside compartment, behind the hinged writing panel, usually was quite elaborate. Its many pigeonholes, letter and storage compartments, and occasional secret compartments gave the artisan an opportunity to apply his talent and his imagination. The man of the house, as the man in charge of this piece of furniture, treasured its many qualities of usefulness. They offered him space for many small pleasures and secrets, for documents, letters or diaries just as for the modest objects he collected, things that played an important role, and with which he liked to surround himself.

Besides the folding front secretary, the **flat top desk** form was also popular. It usually had a cylinder or fall front writing panel, a writing desk with drawers at the sides, often on both sides, and there was a style with a boxy upper section that was set to the back.

Writing desks for ladies achieved a more delicate and ladylike appearance. Generally, they stood free in a room — and so were veneered on all sides — to form an island of cozy intimacy without being isolated from whatever else went on. Also, they could be fitted with expensive features and were admirably suited to contain feminine accessories. Poetry albums, souvenirs of social occasions, or even the letters of a gallant admirer found a worthy place, yet these pieces also offered the chance to work happily. The love of nature, of plants and flowers, was even thought of by the builder of a lady's desk (now at the Austrian Museum of Applied Art in Vienna) which includes two cutouts in the columns to hold flowerpots.

The **showcase** also stood in a special place in the "good room" to contain those romantic, sentimental treasures such as collectible cups, friendship glasses, miniatures or corsages. Often made with glass panels on three sides and a mirrored panel inside, showcases presented the whole range of knick-knacks with pride. Also housed decoratively in them were well-protected porcelain dishes, glasses or silver utensils that only appeared on the table for special occasions or celebrations, under the eagle eye of the lady of the house.

The cases that were somewhat more stable and with a glass panel only in the upper part of the front, leaving more space for decoration as well as structural features, served as **bookcases**. They provided the image of an intellectual attitude, an active life of the spirit, showed an interest in literature and openness to the world, and a desire for education. In addition, the **etagère** and the **servante** were popular with open shelves which also served as places to store or set all kinds of useful things and to hold dishes and baked goods for afternoon tea or coffee hour.

Just as in the eighteenth century, the **commode** still enjoyed popularity. In it, articles of clothing or table settings could be stored away from dust. Deriving from the eighteenth century, the **chiffoniere** developed into a piece of furniture typical of the time. This commode design, extended at the top, often was placed on a wall between two windows.

Highboy commodes and **highboy showcases** formed popular combinations of the two types of furniture named above. They united the utility of a container with proud exhibition in an exemplary manner.

The **wardrobe**, traditional container of all kinds of clothing, was also popular in the Biedermeier era. Larger examples stood in an anteroom or in the hall. The smaller models, with one or two doors, and with proportions more suitable for the user, often found a place in the living area. Often they also included a top drawer at a reachable height. Many imaginative variations took the form of **linen cupboards** with fronts sectioned like a writing desk and equipped with all the corresponding details. Only when one opens the doors, which run the whole width, can they be recognized as linen cupboards. This disguise of a piece of furniture arranged strictly for utilty, for the purpose of making it appear more livable, reflects the results of Biedermeier thinking and documents the vivid imaginations of the era's outstanding artisans.

Their usefulness and optimal use of space made the numerous **corner cabinets** popular. Corner showcases, corner wardrobes, and corner hanging cabinets, often with curved fronts, take the commanding stiffnmess out of the corners of the room, round off the total picture of the space, and create additional possibilities of storage within the limits of the living area.

The life styles of the family members determined personal areas within the space used by all and these "islands of living" were identified by their specific furniture. By this division of roles, **tables** became the unifying meeting points of life. Around them the people gathered, at them they met for the most varied occasions; tables served as meeting places for shared interests and thus became the centers of the culture.

The table was never placed to take up space in the center of the room, but rather was set carefully in the vicinity of the stove, near the wall, or in a corner. It was no longer a purely utilitarian piece of furniture that, as in old days, passed out of sight after a meal when "the board was lifted up". Naturally, tables served as the place to eat meals together, but people also gathered around them for conversations, reading, playing music, or parlor games.

Biedermeier tables usually were round, not indicating any direction, to be accessible from all sides. Many of these tables have a carefully conceived star-shaped veneer pattern on the tops surrounded by a narrow ring of inlay. Built-in drawers or legs attached to the sides, of course, required a design with a wider circular ring. A massive central pillar, which gave a place for decorative shaping, supported the top. Three or four scroll-shaped feet formed a common base, though curved or angular bases were used just as often. There were also combinations of supports including scroll legs, saber legs, column legs, or even legs shaped like dolphins were popular — there seem to have been no limits to the possibilities.

Besides round tables, oval and rectangular **sofa tables** were made in the Biedermeier era, sometimes with folding sides, which were particularly popular in Britain. Semicicular **wall tables**, often with a swinging leg and folding top based on British examples, were made and **card**

tables were built in a similar fashion. The console, in combination with the pillar mirror hanging above it, was no longer as popular as in earlier times because it appeared too fixed in the new arrangement dedicated to mobility.

The interest in furniture mobility is expressed particularly by the large number of exquisite **small tables** that were made in Biedermeier style. They include work, sewing, flower, end, and toilette tables (or pocket-emptiers) with all their special functions, sometimes combining them in one piece of furniture. These small tables catered to the small pleasures and treasured conveniences of modest everyday life. Elaborately equipped toilette tables contain numerous small drawers, compartments, fold-up mirrors, make-up cans, pincushions and space for writing implements. The imagination and cabinetmaking skill of their builders are expressed most impressively in their free, spirited shapes. In addition, the position of the bourgeois housewife in the Biedermeier era was reflected in them, as she lived within the bounds of a homey, apparently happy world, practicing wifely virtues.

Furniture for **sitting** provided neither the stiff seating of the Baroque era nor the coquettish type of the Rococo, nor the equally stiff thrones of the Empire period. The people of the Biedermeier era wanted to sit in comfort without losing stature and dignity. They made an effort to subordinate form, material and design to functionality without losing sight of the desire to create art and a decorative appearance. The unupholstered, open chair backs truly invited decorative designs. Simple bars, bent arches, shaped lyres, segments of circles, vase shapes, carved central splats or three-dimensional dolphins, all this decorated the surface between the chair seat and the crest rail at the top. The latter was given particular attention, for it was supposed to support the sitter's back comfortably with its curved shape. The upholstered seat rested on straight or curved legs at the front and plain squared legs at the back; but they always were set toward each other and thus produced the air of lightness that was desired then.

A lovely alternative to an armchair, easy chair, or bergère was a **wing chair**. The man of the house withdrew into it to rest from the cares and burdens of the day. Adorned with his bathrobe and nightcap, he leaned back, relaxed, and pursued the latest events in the newspapers and magazines. As he nodded over the strenuous events and pleasures, his careworn head found comfortable support on the side "wings" of the chair back. Thus he was caricatured, and thus his era was scoffed at and made into a cliche by following generations.

The **sofa** grew into the definitive Biedermeier seating furniture, the very essence of the age, even pushing the number of individual armchairs into the background. It alone, thanks to its "encompassing" external form, exemplifies the concept of Biedermeier life for it was the shared experiences and feelings that united the middle class, gave it power, and brought it happiness and spiritual inspiration. As the dominant focal point of the seating group, the sofa stood behind the table and offered two or three people a comfortable place to sit for pleasant social togetherness. Then too, it could be used at mealtimes, or it could serve as a handy place for a relaxing pause.

Built wide and inviting, the sofa is delineated by shaped arms and a back that ends at a comfortable height. The arms in particular are often decorated in a variety of shapes ranging from a simple curve to columns, scrolls, rolls, and even to three-dimensional horns of plenty and dolphins. Sitting and leaning surfaces are well-upholstered and often made even softer with cushions and bolster rolls.

As for **benches**, on the other hand, the backs and arms are open and show much of the same artistic decoration as chairs. Small sitting furniture, such as **footstools**, **tabourets** or **ottomans**, completes the large family of seating furniture, which forms probably the most extensive and unified group of Biedermeier furniture.

The variety of furnishings made of wood could be followed on and on in an impressive series, and thus can only be touched upon briefly by mentioning the most typical examples. **Beds** frequently stand in an alcove and are defined by a canopy or draperies. A nightstand is often located in the top end of a bed. **Cradles** display parental pride and joy in their artistic designs. **Hammer pianos** and **spinet pianos** are evidence of an enjoyable musical life; the **giraffe grand piano** with its striking, stretched resonating chamber is one of the most beautiful instruments ever made. **Mirrors** can be found in many forms, from those with simple wooden frames to architectural window facades and standing mirrors known as "Psyche". **Light screens** and **stove screens** often bear effective paintings or are covered with naively artistic embroidery. Along with them, **bobbin boxes** and **workbaskets** were widespread, playing their roles in the devoted production of household goods. Nicely decorated **cuspidors** proclaim the popular habit of tobacco-chewing, decorative **bottle coolers** stand ready for other worldly pleasures, and even **bootjacks** appear in artistic forms.

All of these small pieces of furniture and other furnishings are ultimately lighthearted utility objects which document the significant style of the Biedermeier age.

Designs

In a book about Biedermeier furniture that hopes to provide an overview of the market and simultaneously to be a source of practical advice, perhaps even for the purchase of such a piece, a short introduction to the construction and a description of the original as well as restored condition of the pieces must be presented. Also, in regard to the design, which is just as important to the value of an object as its external appearance, an effort should be made to offer the reader some assistance.

At the beginning of the nineteenth century, furniture material and design took on a greater significance than was the case in the eighteenth century. Their main decoration is usually the carefully selected, lively wood veneer pattern spreading homogeneously over drawers, doors, flaps, and friezes whereby the total impression is disturbed by as few design-related break lines and joints as possible.

In addition, one finds in Biedermeier, especially in the north German coastal area and in north central Germany, elements of Classical architecture that have been incorporated unchanged. Bent or straight-lined elements blend harmoniously into the external sobriety of the object. Defining details seldom occur; rather one senses the ornamentation subordinating itself to the overall appearance.

In most cases, the observer sees furniture of the Biedermeier era at first glance, and the eye does not get lost in details. Perhaps this is the reason the interest of many buyers who previously did not want to get involved with antiques often take to Biedermeier furniture. One hears such reasons as "the furniture does not bludgeon you" or "it harmonizes best with the furnishings", or "I could imagine living with such a piece of furniture". These arguments prove that the appeal of Biedermeier furniture is not as overwhelming as that of furniture from the seventeenth and eighteenth centuries. The size of Biedermeier furniture can be cited as another reason for its popularity. In the early nineteenth century, this furniture was gradually compacted to fit the present customary living conditions.

At the same time, furniture became movable and furthered the new, free spatial art through its versitility. Its livability, comfort, utility and coziness was paramount. The cabinetmaker's intent, thanks to the numerous technical innovations availble to him, was more to the "inner life" of the furniture. At the same time, the external appearance required a high degree of precision, sloppiness could no longer be concealed, as in the eighteenth century, with rich ornamentation.

Any inaccuracy in design and construction that was concealed by refined decor in previous style epochs now became clear to see. In the case of a pre-planned, snugly fitting, undecorated writing panel with a millimeter-wide joint all around, it was simply not possible to add a strip that would conceal any unevenness in this joint. The cabinetmaker could not clean up after a veneer pattern that was continued on all sides of the body.

The demanding precision of the designs required exact workmanship which, because of the few decorative possibilities, resulted in an increased emphasis on technique in furniture making.

Thus it is not surprising that certain innovations in fancy furniture of the late eighteenth century, especially those of cabinetmaker David Roentgen, were quickly adopted in the Biedermeier era. Innovations appeared that are not apparent at first glance, and that give strictly technical advantages, such as improved drawer slides, uncomplicated surface elements, invisible turning techniques, the replacement of turning movements with pushing movements in cylindrical furniture, or the extension of the blind frame construction, etc. Also, technical tinkering, in spite of its nature, served a practical, everyday purpose.

These points make clear that Biedermeier furniture attained a well-deserved place in the history of furniture building.

In order to bring out the fine points of Biedermeier forms, some clarification is needed in advance.

The design of Biedermeier furniture does not give proof of its originality, and many design details are not inventions of the Biedermeier era. But many of the techniques, combinations and design details did not find general use until this style evolved with its emphasis on domestic use and utility.

The characteristic feature of Biedermeier furniture is the cube, a simple box in all its forms, proportions, designs and variations. The means to this feature is through the use of the common wooden board. The board is found in every position and all forms down to the smallest detail of the decoration. The whole piece of furniture is composed of boards carefully worked, and for that reason the board is the outstanding feature of this furniture.

Biedermeier's "true to the material" design style enables one to appreciate the wood by means of precise craftsmanship. No other style in furniture design enables this comprehension in such a clear manner.

Another identifying mark of this style is its "one-sidedness", in which decoration is concentrated on the front. This is particularly noticeable in case furniture but chairs, benches and sofas also have definite front sides and do not make their full impression when seen from the sides; in many cases the full impact can not be observed from that perspective.

For the designing of storage furniture, this meant primarily the board construction of the side areas with precise swallowtail joints, often half concealed, since the corner angles often are closed only with veneer and the area critical to the evenness of the veneering is not, as was often done in the past, surrounded by a base, top or ring profile. This also meant an increase in the dovetailed parts in the dovetailing division, in order to avoid overly wide swallowtail sections and thus also the earlier shrinkage faults. In spite of that, particularly dovetailed and veneered body angles rank today among the areas in which veneer damage, caused by different shrinkage, often appear. In many cases the swallowtails "disappear" into the dovetails, and the resulting difference in height loosens the veneer to almost the same extent, resulting in breakage.

But in addition to the simple, dovetailed board side or top panel, there are also over-veneered frames with plain filling.

Even though it appears more rarely on the actual body, it is often used on the folding panels of writing cabinets or the sliding writing panels of cylinder or roll top secretaries. Here the disappearing of the blindwood is almost without importance for the veneer, which often leads to ugly shrinkage damage on massive surfaces with veneer running in the same direction.

The frame construction was certainly not a cure-all for shrinkage damage of the veneer. But as a rule, it appears in this type of design only when there has been too little moisture in the air of the room.

The technique of squaring off (running the grains of the veneer and the carrier wood at right angles to each other), in which the differing directions of shrinkage are utilized, was used only by chance, if at all, in the Biedermeier era, or when the design absolutely called for it. Thus veneer generally runs vertically on all visible sides. The sides were also made vertical too, running the same way as the veneer; only seldom does one find a commode with veneer running horizontally on the sides, and almost never in blindwood.

As a rule, the grain of the veneer runs lengthwise in board construction. Here a blocking-off effect was likely to be formed with combined or right-angled veneer patterns. Yet with strong shrinkage of the carrier wood, a bulge can develop in the panel, despite the dovetailed angle design. In this case, it can be ascribed to the blocking off. Usually, though, there is a blocking off for the drawers of commodes and writing cabinets. Here the vertical veneer, all united, lies on the horizontally running, half-covered, dovetailed fronts of the drawers. One can often find an inward bulge on these front pieces as a result of shrinkage. In rare cases, brought on by choosing the wrong kind of wood as the carrier, a concave bulge occurs. Even in those days, the rule of thumb for drawer fronts with blocked-off veneer was: the wood side on the inside, meaning the outside of the tree should form the inside of the front board.

Another variation of blocking off veneered surfaces was formed by the veneered leaves of round tables. Here a star-shaped effect came into being, formed by segments of a circle around a midpoint or central field. This circle-shaped arrangement brings about a balanced appearance of the tabletop, as long as the right blindwood is chosen. Often these tabletops, like most massive tops, were also protected against damage by inserted, so-called standing or lying grids. Sometimes too, just a glued-on traversing frieze, repeated at the angles, was used, put on at right angles to the carrier wood to provide this protection.

Blocking off on both sides, such as has come into general use since the beginning of this century with the growth of the plate construction type, was very rare at the beginning of the nineteenth century, and was used exclusively as a means of design. Veneering both sides of the carrier wood, when applied properly, guarantees sturdiness, but at that time this was used only when both optic and aesthetic goals were to be attained simultaneously. Thus one actually finds veneering on both sides only on parts of furniture that are to be seen from both sides, such as writing panels, tabernacle and chest doors, folding lids and folding card-table flaps, and just as often on interior parts of small writing desks, transformable pieces, sewing tables or secretaries.

The top rails of small bars used on oval or round tables can be regarded as an invention of the Biedermeier era. They consist of a ring of wood made of several layers of laminated circle segments. Set back under the edge of the top and vertically veneered all around, they protect the top against damage. This laminated construction is strong and combines a successful optical illusion with high-quality woodworking technique in an impressive manner. In addition to veneering flat surfaces of the sides that show, the Biedermeier cabinetmaker also used other designs that met the demands for functionality, stability and mechanics.

Coping is a fine example of this. As noted above, this was a wooden frieze inserted one to two thirds deep into the wood at right angles to the grain protecting the surface against damage and unifying the breadth, and so providing a wealth of design possibilities. These include leading copings for horizontal movement, including running rails of drawers, copings set into the sides, and refined copings used as running frames with a frieze attached which links the front surfaces between the drawers. Sometimes this running frame is also completed by a similarly attached rear traverse at the back. — This is a case of stabilizing and functional refinement of the design, which first appeared in the developing technology of furniture design in the early nineteenth century, and is often found in Biedermeier furniture.

In more massive form, the coping can appear as the sliding writing panel of a cylinder or roll top secretary or the sliding tablet of a lectern secretary or a richly decorated writing cabinet. It is also used for the fixed and sliding rails (being built in or out) of multi-sectioned built-in compartments which, being enclosed by the hinged writing panel, are part of the interior components of writing cabinets.

The earlier building style using posts continued to be refined. The corner post, a full-length supporting leg and foot to which the entire construction is attached, was used in the eighteenth century, but it withdrew from the vertical contour in the nineteenth century, and in the Biedermeier era disappeared almost completely into the flat surfaces, no longer being recognizable as a carrying element of the design. Therefore, it was possible to make the sides flat and even with the side frames or board sides between them. In the same way, traversing and base friezes, top rails, drawer fronts, folding panels and doors could be made to fit flat. As a constituent of the plane surface, the post no longer had any decorative importance and mainly served to meet the technical requirement for high-quality design. As the high point of this construction, the post, no longer standing out in space, came back into sight thanks to an appropriately formed veneer pattern. The groove — a right-angled guiding groove in comparison to the coping — also took on more importance. In earlier frame construction, panels were set in grooves, but now a rear wall was often inserted into grooves from the bottom; bottoms of drawers were mounted in this way, and even the bottoms of commodes and other small furniture were slid in from the back.

Because the decoration on this furniture was reduced, the board friezes were reinforced, and the long sides of the boards were glued, simple flat massive gluing took on an importance unknown in cabinetmaking until then. Reinforcing and gluing were done in every imaginable way, and the cube grew into space in smaller cubes.

Base feet were reinforced, taking up space, but were kept strictly within the frame of the furniture and often served as the bases for full or half columns, pilasters or stripes, which in turn were only combined in stylized form out of single boards. The simple, all-around base profile is a glued-on board, though often veneered at a right angle in order to bring out a vertical effect. The front framing construction conforms to the shape of the surface, is flat and stepped increasingly or decreasingly, yet simply glued on. Capitals in the form of squares appear to take up just as little space as closing-off upper profiles, which are also formed only from a simple, all-around board forming a plane in front. The side that shows is divided horizontally by steps or mouldings, seldom by vertical breaks in the flat surface, as they would occur in commodes as stylistic remains of formerly curved sides. The flat decoration is limited to simple rectangular or polygonal fields: diamonds, rhombuses and segments of circles — again a layout that, in a strict sense, can be reduced almost completely to the simple board.

On more lavishly built pieces, the crown of the secretary or writing cabinet shows many elements of classic architecture. Here one made use of simple steps. The post was turned into stylized obelisks, the structure was squared, rounded, refined with friezes and copings; everything was plainly glued. The classic frieze, often carried by columns (seldom in profile), closed off the vertical section by lying on the column tops and sidewalls without reaching out into space. As a closing, the flat gable was taken from antique styles and was surmounted in turn by the step gable. In addition, the simple balustrade was a popular edging. All of these elements appear without technical functions, and are dully glued together, so they can be seen as combinations of cut boards.

If there is optical movement in the furniture designs now besides cubic shape, it is always tense, curved and usually on the surface. The movement does not spread out over the contours of the furniture, but remains limited to the outline. The flowing contour of the piece is also under tension. The forms that thus result are in fact new: chair legs are bent and conically shaped, the back is tilted, everything seems to have been created under force. Even the up-turned middle of a chair back seems to have been created under pressure. The changes of form are just as recognizable in the concave base of a console table as in the elliptical or drum-shaped tabernacle crowns of many North German writing cabinets. They can be identified as precisely in the bent-in bars accompanying the central column of a round table as in the "horn-of-plenty" shaped armrests of a sofa.

The round cupola, the spherical body of so-called globe tables, the drum shape or ellipse, the concave shape of sides that show, the arched glass, lyre-shaped feet of sewing tables, and simple curved foot designs

— they all have something in common: they are shapes sawn from a board without taking up space in another direction. In a board, every movement flows to a fixed point without extensions, decorations and changes of direction. Even the round body is made up of boards which are fitted exactly, often vertically braced or assembled into a segmented ring, and then sawn and sanded.

Along with the unique design features in the wood construction of Biedermeier furniture, new technical methods appeared. New types of hardware cut especially to meet the needs of flat surfaces were refined appropriately. The so-called "turning-joint" hinge gained more importance. Because of its focal point in the flat surface and its only attacment in the top wood or cut through to be moved, it works for the flat surface in a unique way. Because of this "invisible" hardware, it was possible to fit precise intermediate moving parts into the flat surface.

Even for the swinging movement of a folding card table, the turning joint was used. Then the card-table design developed for folding surfaces lying one over the other, in which the turning point lies on the symmetrical axis of the two plates, at the joint of the unfolded table. Attached at the edge and invisible from the playing area, it presents a satisfactory technical solution.

Locks were also set into flat surfaces, no longer raised but inset. Thus the technique disappears from the visible area and could be made more compact and thus also could be considerably refined. The lock plate of an inset lock on a writing panel now formed only a delicate technical component of the flat surface. As an inset lock, it even disappeared completely.

Along with the various lock techniques, a detailed description of which would explode the prearranged bounds of this book, we can still mention the advances often utilized for moving parts. Turning and sliding bars were used in the movements of cylindrical secretaries, adaptible furniture, and sometimes in the hidden mechanisms of writing furniture. They transmit power by transfering pushing into turning motion, utilize lever power and the bridging of closing mechanisms.

Athough only particularly elaborately-made furniture was equipped with refinements of this kind, we can still speak of a time when these techniques were refined in the construction of Biedermeier furniture. The cabinetmaker was scarcely able to compete without the cooperation of an appropriate metalworker or the manufacturer of finished parts. Whereas in the past the ability of a cabinetmaker was based almost entirely on his own techniques, which suited the external appearance of the furniture, his expression went straight into the object. Thus, in addition to the appearance and artistic formation of the furniture, often the technical perfection is decisive in the success of these artisans in the first half of the nineteenth century.

Maintaining Value Through Restoration and Care

In a text dealing with furniture, it is important to discuss the basics of restoration before dismissing the techniques, details, and materials.

As a rule, the methods of restoration depend on the attitude of the restorer. To a certain degree, the type of restoration is increased or decreased according to his feelings. But in the end, the results are decisive for the quality of the completed restoration. All too often, the object suffers from the personal attitude of the restorer to the work process that he considers the right one. How much can be ruined in the process by technical incompetence, how much of the original substance can be lost, can be seen over and over in instructive cases.

A restoration should always proceed from the object itself. When the restorer recognizes this and makes himself subordinate to the object, then the most important prerequisites for a proper restoration are in place. Before deciding on a certain method, one must consider the relationship of the restorer to the condition the piece is in. He must choose his methods to correspond with that.

The real task of the restorer is the preservation of the object of art. He conserves it in his preservation and also accepts faults and damage that could be disposed of only through a substantial loss of originality. That means that it must never be the task of the restorer to put the object back into its original condition, giving it a sort of second "new appearance". This is often attempted mistakenly. For thereby the actual condition in which the object exists is falsified, since the object has aged over a certain length of time. Natural traces of aging are just as important and preservable a part of the object as its original appearance. This is true of every fashion trend in the history of furniture, and therefore it goes without saying that the restoration of Biedermeier furniture must be done according to appropriate standards and principles. As in any other style trend, characteristics and innovations in both design and construction came about in the furniture building of the Biedermeier era. The typical characteristics of this epoch, which have already been described elsewhere, naturally have a direct effect on the work of the restorer. Every style trend also includes a great number of characteristic types of damage. For the restorer, this means mastering a series of work processes specifically suited to this era, and their number is not to be underestimated — either in technical or in esthetic terms.

As for the technical side, it seems appropriate to include all the furniture from the late eighteenth century to the end of Biedermeier. In this time period, numerous technical advances became widespread, coming chiefly from France and Britain and making their way to Germany. They were taken up by many cabinetmakers and adapted, until they finally came into general use as new techniques in the Biedermeier era.

In the aesthetic formation and characteristic types of damage linked with it, one must include the Empire furniture that preceded the Biedermeier, particularly in southern Germany. The similar appearance of furniture of these two periods, with large flat surfaces, leads to similar damage, especially to veneered pieces.

For that reason, no special collection of recipes applicable exclusively to Biedermeier furniture can be assembled. Here one should try above all for a protective restoration. In addition, a brief overview of the most commonly occurring dangers and types of damage should be provided, and sensible types of approaches and methods should be introduced.

At the beginning of a restoration, one should always make a thorough examination of the present condition in which the furniture is found. Here the following groups of damage types can be differentiated:

— Damage to the framework of the body, base, doors, tops and drawers.
— Damage to the surface of massively built or veneered pieces.
— Missing pieces and cracks in the framework.
— Missing pieces in the veneer.
— Damage to the surface finish (paint, polish, wax and varnish).
— Damage to the mechanisms, such as bolts, bands, springs, locks and other hardware (exclusively wooden mechanisms are rare).
— Damage to other non-wooden materials, such as colored papering of interiors, leather trim on writing surfaces, cloth, portions of ornamental elements (gilding, polychrome caryatid settings, capitals, feet, etc.)
— Damage to wood inlays or other inlays with tin, brass, mother-of-pearl, ivory and other complex materials.

After checking the condition and determining the damage, the restorer must make a basic decision between conserving and restoring measures.

By conservation we mean maintaining its condition and taking measures that prevent the occurrence of further damage.

Restoration includes the removal of damage. Of course, not every bit of damage to an object must be removed.

Conservation

The most noteworthy form of conserving furniture is attacking the damage done by wood-destroying insects. These are mainly the larvae of the "housebuck" and annobia. The former are capable of destroying the structure of the wood very quickly and almost completely, without the extent of the damage being noticeable at a glance. Often we see an undamaged wooden surface that, remaining paper-thin, conceals the real damage. As for the annobia, the number of so-called exit holes generally allows one to estimate the extent of the damage.

Among the annobia are the "deathwatch" beetle and the various click beetles. High humidity and moderate room temperature are favorable conditions for the development of the larvae, and the emergence takes place between May and August. For that reason, measures taken to combat these pests should absolutely be undertaken earlier, before additional objects are endangered. But it can be determined that a new attack hardly ever occurs in modern apartments, buildings and display rooms, since the climatic conditions are usually not suitable there. But there is always danger of a new attack on unprotected wood from an already attacked object. All the coniferous woods are endangered. In addition, the wood-destroying insects, particularly the annobia, have a preference for animal albumen. For that reason, layers of glue or upper layers of wood under a basis of chalk are usually attacked more strongly than the actual wood.

In combating insect pests, one can either use gas (only done by a specialist!) or injections of a liquid. Liquids include oiling chlornaphthaline wood protection fluids or easily evaporating insecticides like hexachlorcyclohexane and pentachlorphenol. Both of these, too, should be applied only by a restorer, since they can bring on a lot of new damage if wrongly applied. The dangers to health that arise in the process are also very great.

In addition to the combating of wood-damaging insects, a means of solidifying the wood, on account of the destruction of the wood structure, is also used frequently. Nowadays ethyl cellulose and cellulose products are mainly used; they penetrate deeply, with little danger of spreading and thus greater instability as well as inherent tension, and are far better suited to impregnate wood than epoxy or polyester resins.

In addition, there are numerous conserving methods that serve to make the wood firmer. Some strengthen the constructive or massive elements of the body, while others strengthen the veneer of furniture with glued-on elements.

In the body and framework, most damage occurs through brittleness or disintegration of the animal glues used in the first half of the nineteenth century. The brittleness of animal glues develops chiefly from age and changing climatic conditions. In particular, too little moisture in the air encourages this process and ultimately leads to the disintegration of the glue. For that reason, extensive damage to glued joints from dryness often occurs, especially in modern apartments with far too little moisture in the air. Quickly changing amounts of moisture in the air encourage this effect even more, since dampening and drying of the glue can take place very quickly, strongly decreasing its elasticity.

As opposed to becoming brittle, animal glue can also be destroyed by decay bacteria when the humidity of the air is below 65 percent, as can masses joined by glue. The damage is similar to that brought on by brittleness, but it sometimes requires different treatment.

This has two consequences for stabilizing and gluing. It is possible to restore animal glues and increase their binding power with heat and moisture, which does not necessarily make the application of additional glue material necessary, and is also referred to as the "regeneration" of the glue. If the already present amount of glue is not sufficient for this, then the addition of heated glue is necessary. This technique is mainly used to reattach loose pieces of veneer and remove the pockets of air underneath the veneer.

When gluing constructive elements such as bases, sides, frames, attachments, springs and joints, separation of glued joints and other details usually makes a complete regluing necessary, since greater demands are made on the glue. It is an open question as to whether animal or white glue should be used in a given case, since the necessity of making a process reversible when strengthening the framework does not necessarily need to be reversed. The necessity of conserving is of primary importance in this case.

The question of treating the surface is also part of the conserving measures applied to furniture. The original main task in treating a wooden surface is its protection from damage, dirt and climatic influences. Only of secondary importance is the demand for an aesthetic exterior. Thus the surface material can be chosen to unite these two requirements.

The use of waxes and similar materials is known to us today as a very early surface treatment. Only much later were the so-called resin lacquers developed; most particularly in the eighteenth century, ever-stronger combinations of various resins were developed. They have increasing requirements to fulfill in terms of surface protection, color tone, hardness, transparency, ability to be worked and, finally, ability to take a polish. A comparatively modern material is the shellac made of insects from India which has become very widespread — particularly in the Biedermeier era. Its hard surface, quick drying properties (caused by the use of alcohol as a solvent), and relatively quick application resulted in its great popularity at that time.

From the conservative point of view, though, coatings can be applied that, because of their hard finish, offer a good deal of protection from damage in case of changes in climatic conditions, when, especially from dryness, capillary breaks in the polish can result. This shows that the surface is considerably more sensitive to an unfavorable room climate that slowly destroys it. With more elastic types of finish, this occurs much less often and is not as noticeable either.

In this type of surface damage, addition to and polishing over the deadened layer of finish can be of help. In addition, similar and more refined techniques can be tried experimentally in cases of eroding finish damage, large crackled surfaces or light damage (pale, untransparent finish), before the restorer too hastily removes an old layer of finish.

An aged polish or surface is just as much a part of the history of a piece of furniture as the rest of its appearance. Therefore the surface and the finish should receive the same attention as has been applied to paintings and sculptures for many years with the greatest understanding. The restorer must also be clear as to this question, knowing that a removed, even halfway retained surface causes a loss of value, which matters just as much to Biedermeier furniture as to the important earlier pieces of the seventeenth and eighteenth centuries.

Unfortunately, the practice of treating the surface by removing retainable material by the most radical methods, smoothing the wood down and refinishing it is still widespread in present-day furniture restoration. Despite all of this knowledge, such radical measures, now as before, are justified by a higher sale value of the furniture. For that reason it should also be important to the buyer of such furniture to change his concepts of taste in regard to the objects and no longer to advocate spotlessly restored pieces of furniture, as they can be bought new anywhere.

And finally, it must be clear to everyone who cares about art that well-maintained original Biedermeier furniture is becoming rarer all the time, and that this also has an effect on its increasing value.

In the end, every measure, however justified and well carried out, is only of lasting effect as long as the climatic conditions are suitable. Often it is falsely assumed that temperature changes will cause damage to wood, sometimes from dryness. But these depend exclusively on the climatic conditions, which means that the degree of moisture in the air is decisive.

This definitely rises and falls with the room temperature, but it is still possible to have whatever temperatures you want as long as the degree of moisture in the air is kept constant. The ideal range is between 45 and 55 percent. To keep these values comparatively constant during the year and thus to make one's own contribution to conservation as the owner of antique furniture, one requires an air humidifier. As long as the capacity is sufficient, this guarantees the content. In modern heating systems it is simply impossible to create such conditions in any other way. For that reason, measurements of moisture during the heating period usually give values between 20 and 30 percent. This is when the drying damage mentioned above inevitably takes place. Under these conditions, the wood also "works", and thus great damage can result from shrinkage and warping. When one keeps it in mind that wood shrink up to 10 percent in the direction of the grain and up to 5 percent radially (in the direction from the core to the bark) when exposed to moisture from 55 percent to 20, it must become clear that even carefully made designs, which were intended to decrease shrinking damage and eliminate warping, cannot be capable of protecting the furniture from extensive damage.

The following are the most frequently occurring types of damage to Biedermeier furniture:

Warping of massive plates, tearing of glued-together body parts, warping of drawer fronts, shrinkage of fillings in frames (sometimes to the point of falling out), shrinkage of frame elements (which, particularly in the Biedermeier era, were plainly made and veneered over, so that cracks occur along the line of shrinkage), loosening of the veneer from glue deterioration — especially veneered body de signs that suffer characteristic veneer stretching in the case of swallowtail shrinkage in the pins and thus often result in complete detachment.

Biedermeier furniture in particular, on account of its stylistic design and form, is very sensitive to a shortage of moisture in the air. Cracks caused by shrinkage, that occur across the whole of the veneer, are very noticeable and can detract from and falsify the overall appearance. This is usually not so noticeable in, for example, Baroque furniture with rich ornamentation, since shrinkage cracks often appear in deliberate gaps in the veneer.

Aside from artificial humidification, every owner of antique furnishings can take additional measures to avoid damage from shrinkage: no overheating of the rooms the furniture is in (and thus too much moisture removal). Vaporizers and plants both contribute to better moisturization. Furniture should never be placed right next to stoves and radiators; in addition, excessive airing can likewise change the room climate unfavorably. As for the dampness of the outside air, the rule is: winter dry and summer damp.

In every case, airing out the room causes a thorough collapse of the climate, which often leads to inevitable damage. If one always keeps these rules in mind and also prevents overly direct sunlight on the furniture, the prerequisites for the preservation of antique furniture will be considerably improved. For it cannot be in the best interests of the possessor to let the same damage occur to an object again right after restoration. The restorer should not be held responsible for this, for he has no influence over unfavorable climatic conditions. It is more appropriate to become mistrustful when restorers suggest measures by which such damage can be prevented. Uaually these consist of the "impregnation with artificial resins on all sides", "covering with non-yellowing artificial resin finishes", and so on, which are in no way sensible conservatory measures that remain without effects on the substance of the object.

Restoration

The most important purpose of a restorative measure is the removal of blemishes. All sorts of blemishes can be named, including those in the framework, body, exterior, veneer and mounting.

Blemishes in the framework occurred through mechanical influences, including broken-off pieces, other breakage, splintering and the destruction of wood joints, or through use, such as damage to drawers, doors, flaps and other moving parts. These blemishes can usually be removed by making the wood whole. Sometimes too, the replacement or completion of individual parts of the structure is necessary. This applies mainly to foot parts, springs, pegs, runners, drawer bottoms, back walls and bottom grooves of drawers (especially in Biedermeier furniture), dovetail and swallowtail joints, curved pieces of the cylindrical secretaries so beloved in the Biedermeier era, and other construction details, some of which occur more rarely.

In the body, the restorer's primary task consists of removing damage caused by shrinkage. Usually these are cracks in the glued, large-surface body parts or shrinkage cracks of the plain frame elements. This damage often occurs to Biedermeier furniture, and often destroys the appearance of entire sides. If these shrinkage cracks cannot be eliminated by filling adhesives, then usually a strip of wood is set in along the crack. For that reason, the restorer must be very skillful at removing these places of damage. To carry out this work, one also needs a keen eye for the wood color and structure. Every replacement shows up particularly because of the refinishing color, since the impression made by a large flat surface is disturbed considerably when the refinished area shows up clearly. Attempting to eliminate or repair such shrinkage cracks from the rear is very inadvisable if the restored furniture cannot immediately be kept in a controlled climate, for renewed drying and resulting shrinkage in a repaired area encourage cracking in other places. One does better to accept damage in the same place, and thus no other structure will be damaged. Unfortunately, one often sees pieces of Biedermeier furniture with this unwanted problem.

Likewise, runners with holes or scratches should not be glued. This too is often done to prevent shrinkage cracks. This measure is totally ineffective. Shrinkage cracks basically occur because of drying and cannot be prevented in this way.

What with the formation of surfaces that show, already described elsewhere, often traceable back to individual elements like squares, cubes, friezes and other geometrical elements made of wood, the loss of these pieces, which were simply glued on, through external influences on the glue that holds them is very high. If these elements can be reconstructed by the glue traces that show their shapes, then the restorer of Biedermeier furniture can often do cabinetmaking work in the true sense. The requirements in the production of profiles, circle segments, arches, columns, capitals, sawtooth friezes, bases, pedestals, balustrades, legs, feet and many more are very varied and require great skill and sufficient experience to restore expensive furniture.

But there are great demands made on the restorer of Biedermeier furniture in terms of repairing veneer damage too. If the difficulty in restoring decorated models of the eighteenth century is limited to closing bare spots precisely with the right kind of wood, then in these veneer patterns that extend over the entire surface, there is an extraordinary difficulty added: the filling in of gaps must fit quietly and unobtrusively into the often very impressive veneer pattern — particularly on the often-damaged square corners of drawers, traverses, doors and writing panels, just as on wood joints that were so often veneered over. Here too, in addition to the proper operation, good refinishing is a prerequisite for repairs that cause as little disturbance as possible.

Exactly as appropriate measures are necessary for a proper, trouble-free restoration in terms of eliminating wood damage, the surface also depends on carefully made decisions. In the repair of wood damage, every job should be done so that the intact periphery of the damaged place does not become damaged in the process. Cutting too far and smoothing too much, involving the neighboring surfaces, are measures to be rejected out of hand, just as is the general removal of the surface because it apparently cannot be repaired otherwise. Whoever cannot repair wood damage without removing the patina would do better to avoid restoring. Thus arises, after expert repair of all damage, after the carefully considered treatment of the surface involving the usually passively inlaid keyhole shields of ebony, bone or mother-of-pearl, a characteristic large-surface harmony which makes Biedermeier furniture come alive.

When every conserving and restoring measure is suited to the character of the object and the nature of the Biedermeier style is properly understood, and when every measure is carried out with as little loss of material as possible, then the furniture's character and significance to the whole history of furniture is restored by the respectfully working expert. Before beginning any restoration, the restorer must be aware of this important responsibility.

Tips, Trends and Market Tendencies for Biedermeier Furniture

At the time when it was first discovered as a collectors' item — in the nineteen sixties and seventies — Biedermeier furniture was still generally available, and the tendency to acquire the furnishings for a whole room prevailed. Since the beginning of the nineteen nineties, the trend has turned toward striking individual pieces, and above all toward high-quality furniture, usually with elaborate decor, intended to form a deliberate contrast to modern home furnishings. The wish for original furniture with a historically acquired patina is growing, as opposed to the previous preference for complete and often also over-restored furniture.

As for the popularity of various types of furniture, those that were used as containers were traditionally the most popular, since they combined functionality and aesthetics. First we can mention the writing cabinet, but showcases, cabinets and commodes have also been very popular. The writing cabinet — or secretary — offers a wide range of functions, storage space, pleasure in a good-looking "workplace", and good looks in themselves. This also applies to the groups of seating furniture, which consist of a table and appropriate chairs. The pieces of furniture named here usually form the basis and beginning of home furnishings, and over the course of time they were accompanied by small tables, a sofa, armchair, etc., to complete the furnishings.

As for prices, the rule here is just as it is in other areas: Everything that is good is expensive too. Extraordinary and elaborate forms, decoration and masterly workmanship are valued by the buyer, which influences their prices. Furniture of the Viennese School in particular is highly valued on account of these characteristics. Very high prices are generally paid for imaginative single pieces like globe and drum tables, and lyre secretaries. Sets of chairs or ensembles of furniture always sell for more than the sum of the prices paid for the individual pieces. And in addition, original condition always influences the price!

The simple, purely functionally designed furniture is still fairly reasonably priced, as are pieces that need restoration, and neither type needs to be uninteresting. Another factor in pricing is the type of wood used; traditional cherry, followed by walnut, are the most desirable woods. Other woods such as birch, ash and oak are not much in demand, and thus they are often priced more reasonably. Mahogany is not very popular for simpler furniture and thus is priced favorably, but it is very popular for furniture of higher value.

If you want to acquire a piece, you should keep the following in mind as you make a decision:

1. The furniture must appeal to you visually.
2. It should show an original condition of preservation, for replacement parts decrease its value.
3. Make the purchase from either a good specialty shop or at an auction where you can tell from the catalog description what you are getting.
4. Compare various offers before making a purchase.
5. Inform yourself about the cost of possible restoration.

In any case, it is certain that the Biedermeier style has gained a secure place among collectors and lovers of antiques, and its value can continue to grow steadily.

Cabinetmaker's shop, 19th century. Lithograph, circa 1875.

Glossary

Acanthus Leaf-shaped decoration on furniture as also on buildings, named after a Mediterranean plant renowned for its beautiful leaves.

Applique Added decoration.

Arcade Arch or row of arches resting on columns or pillars. A "blind arcade" sections a wall without opening it.

Architrave Element taken from antique architecture, binding two columns horizontally.

Archivolte Element taken from architecture, in the form of the top of a round arch.

Atlant Powerful masculine figure as beam carrier, counterpart to feminine caryatid.

Baluster Rounded, strongly projecting short column.

Balustrade A railing formed with balusters.

Base Columnar foot.

Bastion panel see Bulwark panel.

Beech A very hard wood, used for chair and cabinet legs and simple pieces of furniture.

Bergère 18th-century form of seating furniture with full upholstery and closed arms, usually with loose seat cushions.

Beveled In furniture, the angling of the rim of a framed panel or inset glass.

Biedermeier style The first middle class decorative style, widespread in Austria and Germany, and as far north as Sweden, between 1815 (early Biedermeier era) and 1848 (late Biedermeier era).

Blind An architectonic motif added to a body for decoration and sectioning (such as a blind arch or arcade).

Blindwood The secondary (carrier) wood to which veneer is glued.

Bulwark panel Richly figured paneling resembling a bird's-eye view of fortifications, also known as bastion paneling.

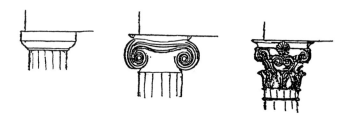

Capital The upper part of a column, pillar or pilaster, extending out over it.

Cartonnier A small chest of drawers for writing implements, set onto a writing desk.

Caryatid A feminine statue used as a carrier in place of a column, counterpart of a masculine Atlant.

Channeling Sectioning of flat surfaces by vertical grooves, usually found in pillars and columns.

Cherry Brownish to red-brown hardwood, often with a nice grain, especially used for veneer in the Biedermeier era.

Chiffoniere A pillared chest of drawers, tall slim chest with numerous drawers, usually placed in front of pillars between windows.

Classicism Artistic trends imitating antique classic styles, including the period from about 1770 to 1850. The phase before 1800, in which Louis XVI elements lived on, is called "Directoire" after the revolutionary Directory. The next two decades were generally called "Empire" on the Continent, after the empire of Napoleon. Roman, Greek and Egyptian motifs appear as decorative elements.

Despite Napoleon's efforts to inspire many branches of commercial art, these art forms suffered a decline during the Revolution and Napoleonic Wars. The strongest type proved to be the making of furniture, The Biedermeier style grew out of this trend.

Collar The projection of a piece out of a flat surface.

Column A round vertical support consisting of base, shaft and capital.

Column sectioning Division of a column into base, shaft and capital.

Conifer Long-grained softwoods such as spruce, fir and pine, particularly used for early and rustic furniture in South Germany and Apline regions, later usually used as blindwood.

Cornice An S-shaped profiled moulding.

Corpus The body of storage furniture, but also the plain, unseen blindwood of veneered furniture.

Crotch veneer Veneer made by cutting through the places where a tree trunk branches.

Crown An element closing off the vertical extent of a piece of furniture at the top (such as an acanthus crown).

Crosscut Wood cut at right angles to the grain.

Cylinder bureau A writing table divided by a jalousie or flap into half- or quarter-cylindrical shape, made in Germany and Austria around 1750 and also popular in the Biedermeier era. When opened, the jalousie rolls between the back wall and sliding box; when the cylinder is pushed back, the writing surface comes forward. This design is said to be promoted by Count Kaunitz, thus it is also known as a "Bureau à la Kaunitz" or simply a "Kaunitz".

Cyma A decorative moulding (*kymation*, Greek wave) of curving shapes.

Diamond band An ornamental band with a row of diamond shapes.

Doubling Reinforcing, gluing boards together with grains at right angles to hinder cracking and parting of the wood.

Drum chest A chest of drawers in the form of a large drum, similar to a column commode.

Ebonist A worker in ebony, used since the 17th century to mean an art cabinetmaker producing luxury furniture.

Ebony Various dark, heavy and hard exotic woods, used for expensive furniture in the 16th and 17th centuries because of its ability to take a high polish.

Egg & Dart moulding Antique decorative band of alternating ovoid and pointed forms, usually bordered by pearl staffs.

Empire Style Classic art style, 1800-1820, introduced by architects P. F. L. Fontaine (1762-1853) and Ch. Percier (1764-1838) in their pattern book *Recueil de la décoration interieur*; also can include the style period called "Directoire" after the Directory period (1790-1800) of the French Revolution. While the Continent used the name on account of Napoleon's reign, the British called this period (1811-1820) the Regency, as George IV was then regent for his father George III. Since the silhouette of the usually elegant furniture is strict, clear, simple and usually straight-lined, decorations usually show Egyptian, Greek and Roman motifs (sphinxes, griffins, winged steers, lions, horses, urns, wreaths, garlands), while ornaments like the meander and the egg stripe are also used on the surfaces of ornate, usually mahogany-veneered furniture.

Etagère Set of shelves open on all sides. with intermediate shelves open on three sides, free-standing or set on a piece of furniture.

Fan A part of a rosette or other popular decorative motif taken from Renaissance architecture.

Festoon A decorative motif in the form of a garland, or an arched hanging of flowers, leaves or fruit, often wound crosswise with bands, usually with bands at both ends.

Fiale A slim, pointed tower, often used as a decorative motif in Gothic style.

Filet Diagonal light and dark bands of veneer, usually used as a frieze.

Fluting A concave cutout, especially in mouldings, profiles and frames.

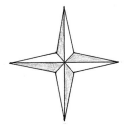

Folded star A star-shaped inlay with a three-dimensional effect created by light-dark contrast.

Frame design Construction type used in central Europe since the Middle Ages, in which a frame of square pieces is finished with fillings. The thin filling pieces enough play in the grooves of the framework that the wood can expand without breaking.

Frieze Thin flat stripes, usually used to edge or enclose a flat surface, with ornamental or figured decor.

Furniture The variety of furnishings developed for living and storing. Unlike most movable (mobile) furniture, individual types are built into a room.

Gable A rooflike closing on a piece of furniture.

Gable field Facade surface of a gable, often ornamented or decorated with reliefs.

Garland see festoon.

Graining Patterns made by using various directions and tones of wood grain. Coniferous wood is very nicely grained, as are walnut, birch and ash. Root furniture made of wood from the lower areas of tree trunks shows a particularly lively grain pattern.

Grain veneer Crosscut veneer with a particularly lovely clouded pattern.

Groove Lengthwise channel in which a wooden part is fitted at right angles to its attachment. Tongue and groove were the prerequisites of furniture building.

Gueridon A small, high, usually round decorative table.

Hairline inlay This strips of intarsia or other inlay, forming a light-dark contrast.

Half-column or **three-quarter column** A column projecting only halfway or three quarters of the way out of the wall (see column, pillar, pilaster).

Hardwood The tree's inner woods used for veneer and inlays because of their beauty and value.

Historicism The pluralism of styles that dominated the latter half of the nineteenth century. In the 1840's, Gothic style elements experienced a rebirth in all of commercial art and architecture. This was called Neo-Gothic, and resulted in individual pieces of furniture as well as buildings. The "Neo- Baroque" was very productive in terms of furniture production. Countless objects from the mid-nineteenth century are still on the market today. Centers of their production led to the names "Dresden Baroque" or "Viennese Baroque". In the eighteen seventies and eighties, the Neo-Renaissance, also known in Germany as "Old German Style", followed.

Horn of plenty A horn, usually twisted, filled with flowers, fruits and the like, used as a symbol of richness and plenty.

Intarsia Inlay work of various pieces of colored wood or other materials, set in a panel of wood, as opposed to marquetry.

Interior The arrangement of numerous drawers, shelves and pigeonholes behind the outside doors of writing and storage cabinets.

Joint In the course of its history, the cabinetmaker's art has developed numerous ways of joining pieces of wood, with nails, screws, glue, etc., as well as interlocking or pegging. Holes of the same size are drilled in two pieces and wooden pegs are driven through them, or one piece is cut positively and the other negatively so that they interlock exactly. In swallowtail joints, the two pieces are joined so that projections in one fit into cutouts in the other. Boards are also joined by tongue and groove. Dovetails and numerous other means of joining have also been used.

Knee joint Projecting, multiangled form of a moulding.

Louis XVI Style Named for the reign of Louis XVI (1774-1792), but beginning as an artistic style around 1760. National names such as "Queue Style" in Germany never became popular. Unlike the previous Rococo, the form of furniture became stricter and was based on Classic influences, including antique ornaments like coin chains, wave and meander bands, festoons and symbolic decorations. The decoration, particularly intarsia, was further refined, and many renowned ebonists such as David Roentgen tried to outdo each other with clever multipurpose furniture. Unlike more lavish furniture, the bouregeois Louis XVI has a simple elegance.

Lyre Popular furniture motif from Louis XVI style to Biedermeier, used on chair backs, bottoms of sewing tables, etc. There were also secretaries in lyre form.

Mahogany An exotic wood imported since the late 17th century and used particularly for veneering, since it does not loosen and takes a high polish. First used in France, Britain and North Germany, it found acceptance all over Europe in Louis XVI style and became especially popular in the Empire era.

Marquetry Inlay work using variously colored wood or other materials in veneer, as opposed to intarsia.

Masks Decoratively used masks as a three-dimensional decorative element.

Meander An ornamental band, taken from antique times, made of a line broken by right angles.

Moulding A horizontal, extending, usually profiled element of furniture design, used to section a piece of furniture, or as an upper or lower closing in simple or stepped, profiled form.

Mussel shell An often-used motif of the Renaissance and Baroque or Rococo.

Oak Widespread hardwood, pale brown to yellow-brown, with clearly marked pores forming lines; one of the hardest woods, used in massive, naturally pale form, etched, waxed, or veneered as blindwood, rarely used as veneer.

Oxhead chair A Biedermeier chair with a narrower back than the shovel chair, without a tongue.

Palmette Vegetable-like ornament of symmetrical leaves in a fanlike pattern.

Paneling Thin boards that are fitted into a frame with grooves so they can move without breaking.

Pearl staff Decorative motif of small pearl-like balls in a row, sometimes used as upper and lower borders of an egg-and dart moulding.

Pier A flat, usually narrow vertical projection of a wall, without base or capital, to section a surface.

Pilaster A flat wall pillar that, like a column, consists of base, shaft and capital, unlike a pier.

Pillar An angled upright, as opposed to always round columns, also a round upright without base or capital.

Pillow filling Elegant pillow-shaped filling.

Pine Coniferous softwood.

Polychrome multicolored, colorful.

Portico An entry with roof supported by columns.

Post Vertical round or squared wood with a carrying function.

Prie-Dieu Small cabinet to hold prayer and hymn books, combined with a kneeling pad.

Profile In furniture, this concept includes mouldings of varying forms. Flat mouldings are planed to produce a profile.

Profile plane A cabinetmaking tool with which, by inserting various blades, profiles can be planed into mouldings.

Psyche In furniture, a rotating standing mirror in a frame, widespread in Empire and Biedermeier styles.

Queue style A derogatory name for German art between 1760 and 1780, corresponding to Louis XVI style, and named for the prevailing men's hair style of the time.

Relief Latin *relevare*, to raise up, figures or ornamental designs raised above a flat surface.

Restoration The art of restoring furniture.

Rosewood A hard, easily-worked exotic wood, dark brown to violet, with deep black veins when cut lengthwise.

Scale veneer Since the 19th century, veneer is no longer sawn but "scaled" off a turning log, making it possible to reduce the veneer's thickness considerably, in some cases down to 0.05 mm.

Secretary A popular writing desk derived from those used in Italy in the 17th century and in Louis XVI and Empire styles, with a central panel folding out forward to form a writing surface, and usually an interior of many drawers and pigeonholes. The top of the piece has a narrow drawer, and the bottom can be made as a cabinet with doors or a commode with drawers.

Servante A cabinet (with mirror in the back) in which to display decorative objects.

Shaft The long central section of a column, with a capital at the top and a base at the bottom.

Shovel chair Typical Biedermeier chair with shovel-shaped back, wide at the top, ending in stylized scrolls at the sides, and with a descending splat in the middle.

Sofa Seating furniture introduced at the end of the 17th century, under Turkish influence, with back and arms, holding up to six people.

Splat The middle piece in the frame of a chair back or a surround, often ornamentally shaped.

Spruce A long-fibered coniferous softwood used only in rural furniture as secondary wood, for interior parts such as drawers, etc.

Squaring off Design to prevent crack formation in veneer, by reducing movement of secondary wood to a minimum by setting grains at right angles to each other.

Staff A thin vertical member, used in Gothic style as lower members of a window frame with an arched field of tracery.

Stop moulding Moulding that covers the crack between cabinet doors or between a door and the frame, striking against the other door or the frame when the door is closed.

Style Furniture of a later era that uses stylistic features of an earlier era, as in Historicism.

Stretcher A horizontal connection between posts, usually a thin hanging edge, as under a table top, a skirt at the bottom of a cabinet or commode, or a support under the seat of a chair or sofa.

Swallowtail Cabinetmaking corner joint in which conical pieces fit together.

Tabouret A low, upholstered stool on four legs, used since about 1700.

Tongue A construction detail used in wood corner joints and fitting into a groove.

Dental moulding Antique decorative moulding used in furniture, made of a row of small projecting blocks separated by narrow gaps, a type of frieze.

Tracery Gothic decor based on the circle, an abstract geometrical ornament without illustrative meaning.

Veneer Thin sheets of wood with which the simple secondary wood is covered, or the act of covering the secondary wood with veneer.

Volute A rolled pattern used on furniture, often as transition between horizontal and vertical members.

Wainscoting Covering walls or ceilings with wooden paneling.

Walnut Popular hardwood used in 17th- and 18th-century in German and French cabinetmaking. Cut along the grain, it provides the usual light brown veneer with blackish veining. Crosscut, it provides grained veneer with black cloudy pattern. If the inner core is sawn across the grain, the dark root-grain veneer is obtained. Walnut is usually used as veneer. It bleaches in strong sunlight.

Window Seat A sofa without a back and with angled arms.

Writing cabinet Also called a tabernacle secretary, with lower section like a cabinet or commode and usually a gabled top (with a closing section and drawers); in between is a middle section with small drawers and an angled front panel that folds down to form a writing surface. Made in Britain in the early 18th century, it became the most widespread type of men's furniture in Rococo Germany.

Writing commode Commode used in the late 18th century, having an uppermost drawer with a folding front panel that forms a surface for writing. Later the folding drawer was replaced by a small structure with an angled writing panel.

Notes on Photos and Prices

When one concentrates on a single stylistic epoch in putting together a book on furniture, it is advisable to set up a system corresponding to the various types of furniture. The table of contents also gives an overview of the illustration section. For every label word, as broad a spectrum of the existing types of furniture as possible should be shown with brief descriptions of their characteristics. Special terminology is explained in the glossary. Often, though, the meaning of a specialized term becomes clear through looking at both the definition and the illustration or illustrations.

In every kind of catalog, the value of the information is of paramount importance. For many readers, the price guide will hold the most important information. Just comparing the values of a single type of furniture shows that what appear to be very similar pieces can be evaluated very differently. This is because there are only "similar" and not "like" pieces on the one hand, and no "like" buyers on the other. And precisely these two factors lead ultimately to a price: supply and demand.

To attain a certain balance in the price guide, prices paid for furniture at auctions are stressed. Since the prices paid for these pieces are arrived at in open bidding, they seem realistic, but this does not exclude the possibility that far higher prices could be paid under different conditions by a collector who simply had to have a long-sought piece. The fact that such exceptions sometimes occur at auctions too is shown by, among others, the case of the lyre secretary shown in color, which was sold for about 90,000 Marks at an auction. Naturally, undervaluings can take place at auctions too, when—as, to be sure, has rarely happened with Biedermeier furniture in recent years—only one bidder appears in the auction room and no competition materializes.

The prices charged in the trade are something very different. Here a great number of, in some cases, high-quality individual pieces are assembled and kept on hand by specialists for a certain stratum of buyers who want to compare and find perfectpy restored pieces. Costly work on the pieces and sometimes long storage periods must be paid for by the selling price. The customer has the pleasure of not having to decide under pressure of time, of being served on an individual basis, and of having the purchased object delivered or even being able to have it inside his own four walls for a trial period.

As a rule, an auction house cannot offer such services, which generally results in more reasonable prices. Since every dealer sets his prices by his own methods, the prices charged in the trade are very subjective, which, on account of its unevenness, is less suitable for use in a price guide. It would only add to the reader's confusion and obscure clearer information. The user is served better by a set of figures that originated publicly and thus are more uniform and objective, than by citations whose origins he would have to investigate. To be sure, he must be sure that, under certain conditions, specific additions must be made to the prices.

To make clear that the evaluation of antiques is flexible, a price range will be cited rather than a single price.

And one thing must not be forgotten: Trends, like fashion changes, personal feelings, international market fluctuations—all of these influence what happens—and finally, the entire art business goes by the rule of thumb, "A work of art is worth what people will pay for it." Seen in this light, the price guide is to be regarded simply as a guide and not as a price list. For the illustrations we thank the sources cited in the photo credits.

*Karl Begas, **The Begas Family**, 1821, Wallraf-Richartz Museum, Cologne.*

F 1a

F 1b

F 1 a+b Various pieces of furniture and furnishings on sale at an auction.

F 2 Bookcase, walnut, 157 x 108 x 49 cm. German, ca. 1830. $6,000-8,000.

F 3 Writing cabinet *with mirrored interior and painting. Mahogany, unrestored.*
182 x 108 x 55 cm. Central German, ca. 1820. $8,000-10,000.

F 4

F 4 Showcase, *glazed on three sides, with mirror in back. Black, polished, partly gilded. 170 x 103 x 51 cm. Probably Viennese, ca. 1820. $12,000-13,500.*

Armchair *with shovel back, arms ending in birds' heads. Ash rootgrain, 99 cm high. Vienna, ca. 1820. $5,250-6,500.*

F 5

F 5 Writing cabinet, *black, polished. 150 x 100 x 44 cm. Viennese, ca. 1815, $20,000-24,000.*

F 6

F 6 Twin Beds with painted panels, walnut, partly marbled. 151 x 197 x 93 cm.
Austrian, ca. 1825. $10,000-12,000.

F 7

F 7 Secretary, *walnut with painting, unrestored. 199 x 126 x 60 cm. Central German, ca. 1815. Over $30,000.*

Chair, *Empire style. $3,500-4000.*

F 8

F 8 **Writing Cabinet** *with a cabinet on top. Formerly organ works were in the cabinet. Cherry, unrestored. 211 x 120 x 64 cm. West German, ca. 1820. Over $25,000.*

F 9 **Wardrobe**, *cherry. 204 x 176 x 57 cm. Swabian, ca. 1825. $8,000-10,000.*

F 9

F 10 Lady's Secretary, walnut. *134 x 72 x 35 cm. Viennese, signed Josef Schwab, dated 1816. Over $50,000.*

F 11 Writing Cabinet with mirrired interior, grained walnut. *156 x 108 x 51 cm. South German, ca. 1815-1820. $20,000-25,000.*

F 10

F 11

F 12

F 12 Table, mahogany, with inventory
stamp of Duke Ernst II of Saxe-Coburg
and Gotha. 72 cm high, 115 cm diameter.
Central German, ca. 1830. $6,000-8,000.

F 13

F 13 Extension Table, walnut, 78 cm high, 116 cm diameter. German, ca. 1820. $13,500-15,000.

F 14

F 14 Servante, mahogany. 175 x 95 x 52 cm. Viennese, ca. 1815. $25,000-30,000.

F 15 Showcase, mahogany. 149 x 93 x 50 cm. Saxon, ca. 1820. $10,000-12,000.

F 15

F 16

F 16 Worktable with sliding side panels,
cherry. 81 x 85/159 x 52 cm. South German, ca. 1825. $8,500-10,000.

F 17

F 17 Pyramid Chest of drawers, *cherry.*
78 x 103 x 52 cm. South German, ca. 1825.
$9,500-12,000.

F 18

F 19

F 18 Set of four tabourets, *mahogany. 58 cm high. German, ca. 1820. $6,500-8,000.*

F 19 Sofa, *cherry. Viennese, ca. 1820. Over $12,000.*

F 20 Tea table, *solid ash with line inlay. 76 cm high, 83 cm diameter. South German, ca. 1820-25. $3,500-4,500.*

Set of four chairs, *massive ash, line intarsia. South German, ca. 1825. $8,000.*

F 21

F 22

F 21 Sofa *on a central foot, fully upholstered, movable, maple and mahogany veneer on spruce. 100 x 194 x 70 cm. Vienna, circa 1820. Over $25,000.*

F 22 Sofa, *walnut. 103 x 203 x 71 cm. Mainz, signed Anton Berger, dated October 12, 1830. $10,500-14,000.*

F 23 Pillar cabinet, *with ornamental inlay, cherry. South German, circa 1825. $6,500-10,000.*

F 24 Shear chair, *cherry, height 72 cm. South German, circa 1820. $5,500-7,000.*

F 25 Cradle, *cherry with cloth lining, circa 1820-25. $4,750-6,500.*

F 26 Servante *with mirror or rear wall, pear, polished black, partly gilded. Viennese, circa 1815-20. Over $30,000.*

F 23

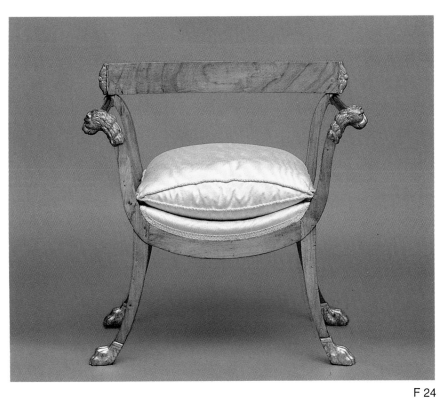

F 24

F 25

F 26

F 27 a-c Six-piece set, mahogany, with original upholstery. Viennese, probably by Josef Danhauser, circa 1820. Over $30,000.

F 27a–c

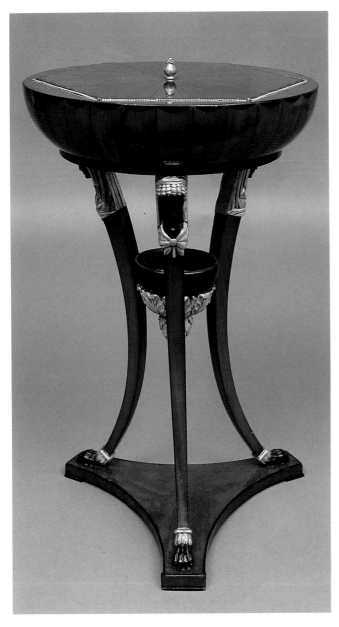

F 28

F 28 Drum table, *mahogany, 74 cm high, 46 cm diameter. Viennese, circa 1815. Over $40,000.*

F 29 Globe table, *mahogany, 99 cm high, 55 cm diameter. Central German, circa 1820. Over $35,000.*

F 30

F 30 Pyramid secretary, birch, 183 x 96 x 47 cm. Leipzig, circa 1820-25. Over $32,000.

F 31 Pyramid writing cabinet in beautiful historical condition, mahogany. Central German, circa 1815-20. Over $40,000.

F 31

F 32

F 33

F 32 Lyre secretary, *mahogany, carved parts gilded. Central German, Hannover, circa 1815. Over $65,000*

F 33 China closet, *glazed on three sides, cherry veneer on fir. South German, circa 1825. $10,000-12,000.*

F 34

F 34 Cabinet, *cherry. 83 x 101 x 54 cm.*
Probably from Munich, circa 1820.
$16,500-20,000.

F 35

F 35 Salon table, *walnut and birch. 79 x 93 x 64 cm. Viennese, circa 1815-20. Over $20,000.*

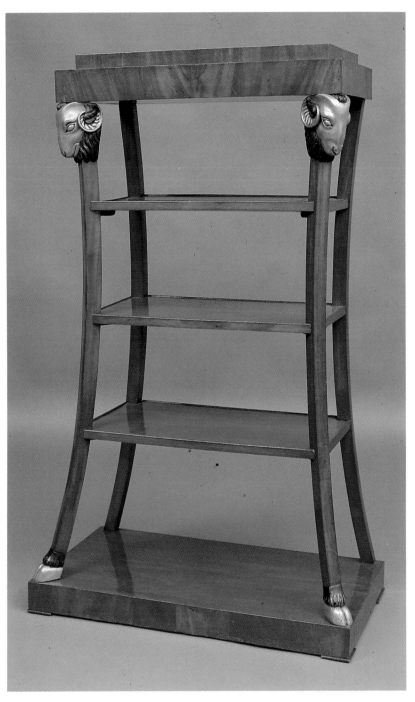

F 36

F 36 Etagère, mahogany. 143 x 74 x 38 cm. Viennese, circa 1820. Over $16,500.

F 37

F 37 Roll top desk, *pear. 148 x 101 x 58*
cm. Southwest German, circa 1825.
$12,000-15,000.

F 38

F 38 Sewing cabinet, *mahogany. 30 x 30 x 19 cm. North German, circa 1820. $5000-6,500.*

F 39

F 39 Lyre secretary, *with mirrors inside, secret compartments, walnut veneer on spruce. 185 x 106 x 57 cm. Austria-Hungary, circa 1830. Over $50,000.*

Gallery of Illustrations

Highboy Secretaries

The highboy secretary lost importance with the beginning of Classicism, and turned up only occasionally in Biedermeier furnishings. The most striking change in its design is the replacement of the straight writing panel with a quarter-round roll top, which opens automatically when the writing panel is pulled out and reveals a usually lavishly appointed secretary section. Rich decoration and lavish facilities, sometimes including secret compartments, make it highly valuable.

1

2

1 Cylinder Highboy Secretary on green paw feet. Sliding writing panel with automatically opening quarter-round enclosed writing area, display cabinet with double glass doors on top. Cherry with birch grain-stripe veneer on oak. 222 x 122 x 68 cm. South German, circa 1815-20. $12,000-16,000. Early example, veneered with cherry, very much in demand today.

2 Cylinder Highboy Secretary on tapered square feet. Three-door top with projecting central part, crowned by gable profile and ornamentally pierced gallery. Walnut half- and matched grain veneer on spruce. 199 x 118 x 64 cm. South German, circa 1820. $8,000-10,000.

Caspar Obach (*Zürich, 1807-1868, Stuttgart*), **Salon of a Stuttgart House circa 1840**, *watercolor. Peter Griebert Gallery, Grünwald near Munich.*

Bedroom, *Auersperg Palace, Vienna, 1814.*

3

4

3 Cylinder Highboy Secretary. *The uppermost sliding panel made for writing, with two sliding drawers and a folding writing panel in the center. Secretary interior with numerous pigeonholes with central architectural layout and secret compartment. Etched grained birch. 196 x 112 x 54 cm.*
North German, circa 1825. $6,500-8,000.
Characteristic of northern Germany is the often three-doored, clearly stepped top section with the gable crown.

4 Cylinder Highboy Secretary *with opened writing area, on typical bracket feet adopted from Britain. Pyramid mahogany. 204 x 120 x 57 cm.*
North German, circa 1825. $6,500-8,000.

Bracket feet are board feet with a straight outer angle and curved inside contours.

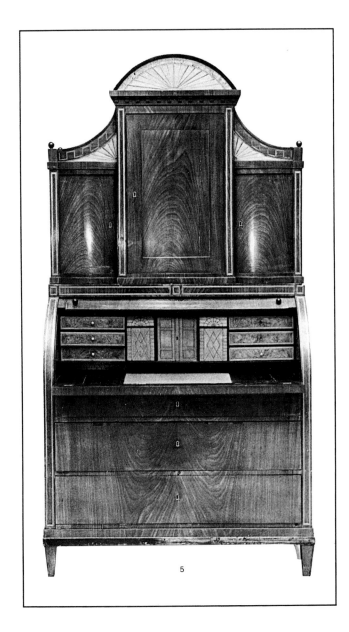

5 Cylinder Highboy Secretary. *Stepped three-door top with straight central section and convex side boxes. The crown takes the form of contrasting circle segments with stylized shell ornamentation and meander bands at the sides.*
Mahogany. 228 x 110 x 58 cm.
North German, circa 1820. $8,000-10,000.

The shell ornamentation was a very popular decoration in Britain which was adopted and often used, especially in northern Germany.

6 Cylinder Highboy Secretary. *Three-door top with straight central section, bowed sides and gable crown.*
Mahogany. 203 x 111 x 52 cm.
North German, circa 1820. $6,500-8,000.

7 Cylinder Highboy Secretary. *Writing section with architecturally formed inlays and secret compartments. Stepped top above, the central part divided into compartments and folding out to form a lectern.*
Mahogany. 228 x 128 x 66 cm.
North German, circa 1825.$6,500-8,000.

An interesting detail is the top part that folds out to form a lectern, allowing short-term writing from a standing position.

8 Cylinder Highboy Secretary. *Curved top section, blending in at the sides, made as a writing compartment.*
Ash. 202.5 x 114 x 57.5 cm.
Denmark, circa 1825-30. $4,750-6,000.

In comparison, furniture with ash veneer has lower values.

9

10

9 Roll top Highboy Secretary. *Lower part with three drawers on each side, covered by doors. The writing area and the middle door above have tambour closings.*
Mahogany. 159 x 117 x 74 cm.
North German, circa 1820. $6,750-8,000.

The cylinder is replaced here by a lighter roll top.

10 Roll top Highboy Secretary. *Lower part includes nine drawers, open kneehole with two doors. Top has folding-out lectern and secret compartments.*
Mahogany. 217 x 132 x 94.5 cm.
North German, circa 1830-35. $4,750-6,000.

Highboy Showcases

With this type of furniture, one must make sure that the chest of drawers bottom and showcase top originally were made to go together. Proportional balance, correesponding shape, unified choice of wood and grain and harmonious surface should be the identifying marks to indicate that the parts were originally together. Otherwise, they are said to be "married".

12 Highboy Showcase. Three-drawer chest of drawers section, showcase top with two glazed frame doors. Black painted columns with bronze capitals and bases.
Cherry. 195 x 115 x 58 cm.
South German, circa 1820. $6,800-8,000.

In the Biedermeier era, drawer handles and keyhole shields were almost always made of thin sheet brass that was stamped over a model. If they and the locks, as in the illustrated example, are still original, they justify a somewhat higher price.

11 Highboy Secretary. The plate of the lower section has two folding supports for the fall front writing surface. Two glazed doors above.
Cherry, 185 x 105 x 53 cm.
South German, circa 1835. $3,750-4,750.
Simple rural secretary, correspondingly moderately priced.

13

14

13 Highboy Showcase on bowed square legs. Top showcase with two drawers below glazed double doors. Original stamped brass hardware.
Cherry. 175 x 126 x 63 cm.
South German, circa 1820-25. $5,250-6,500.

14 Highboy Showcase on square feet below columns. Glazed showcase top with gable crown. Ebonised keyhole shields shaped like shields.
Cherry. 220 x 115 x 62 cm.
South German, circa 1820-25. $6,800-8,000.

In the Biedermeier era, metal fittings were often eliminated. The carefully selected and applied surfaces of wood grain were to be the only decoration. The keyhole shields, usually made in the form of shields and set into the wood, best suited this requirement. They were ebonised, painted black to resemble the desired and expensive ebony wood.

15

16

15 Highboy Showcase *on post feet with blocks. Showcase above with with moulding at the top.*
Cherry. 179 x 133 x 63 cm.
South German, circa 1830. $3,500-4,000.

The later time of origin and simpler design explain the price difference from the other examples.

16 Highboy Showcase. *Prismatic chest of drawers section on replaced baluster feet. Showcase above with mirror on back wall. Edge bands set off in black on all sides.*
Cherry, 191 x 122 x 62 cm.
South German, circa 1825. $3,500-4,500.

The later baluster feet must be regarded as lowering the value.

17 Highboy Showcase. *Two black-painted round columns flank the three-drawer chest of drawers body and support the slightly projecting top drawer. Showcase with single door and glass on three sides.*
Cherry, 192.s x 102 x 59 cm.
South German, circa 1820. $4,750-6,000.

18 Highboy Showcase. *Three-drawer chest of drawers section, rounded on the sides. Showcase above with gable. Cherry. South German, circa 1830. $3,500-4,500.*

19

20

19 Highboy Showcase. *Narrow form, decorated in front, show-case with single door and glass on three sides. Original hard-ware with a pair of doves above an urn vase.*
Cherry, 176 x 59 x 40 cm.
South German, circa 1825. $4,000-5,250.

20 Highboy Showcase. *Lower section with single door, inset arch pattern, and paw feet. Showcase with glass on three sides, flanked by round columns with gilded Corinthian capitals.*
Mahogany. 184 x 86 x 50 cm.
Circa 1815. $6,750-8,500.
Early highboy showcase with harmonious proportions.

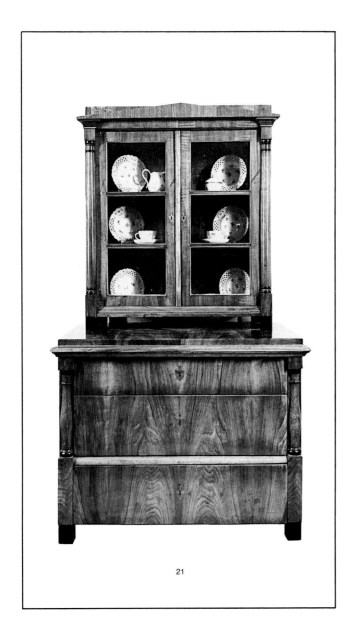

21

22

21 Highboy Showcase. *Chest with three drawers, the bottom one slightly projecting. Showcase above with two glazed and decorated frame doors, projecting gable.*
Walnut. 180 x 107.5 x 63 cm.
Circa 1820-25. $5,250-7,000.

22 Highboy Showcase. *Two-door prismatic lower part, its projecting, profiled plate wreathed by a decorative balustrade. Showcase above with pseudo-Gothic tracery crown.*
Walnut. 196 x 120 x 58 cm.
Circa 1820-25. $3,250-5,000.

Pseudo-Gothic decorative elements were occasionally used for decoration even in the early days. The doors show typical shrinkage cracks, such as appear on large surfaces when there is too little dampness in the air.

23

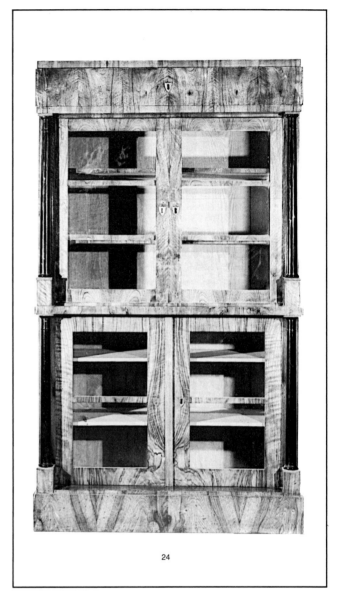

24

23 Highboy Showcase. *Four-drawer chest, matching two-door showcase above with stepped top and additional drawers. Walnut, fine edge stripes of maple, ornamental inlaid fields of cherry. 175 x 78 x 55 cm.*
Circa 1825. $3,500-5000.

24 Highboy Showcase. *Lower part and showcase as mirror-image basic forms with glazed and trimmed frame doors. The base part corresponds to the top, the latter includes a drawer. Walnut.*
South German, circa 1820-25. $4,000-5,500.

Cabinets

25 Highboy Showcase. *Chest of drawers body rounded at the sides, with curved plate on scroll feet. Patterned fillings on glazed top, sawn silhouette on top board.*
Elm. 206 x 123 x 69 cm.
Circa 1840. $2500-3,500.

The curved elements used here are characteristic of the late time of origin.

26 Console Cabinet. *Half-round (demi-Llne) shape with door and top drawer on curved and tapered square feet.*
Cherry. 82 x 58 x 36 cm.
South German, circa 1820-25. $3,500-4,000.

Interesting, and typical of the Biedermeier era, is the formal reshaping of the console table, intended purely for decoration, into a more purposeful storage cabinet.

27 Console Cabinet *with flanking round columns.*
Birch. 82 x 79 x 47 cm.
North German, circa 1825. $3,000-4,000.

28

29

30

31

32

33

28 Console Cabinet with drawer at the top. Walnut. 93.5 x 70 x 37.5 cm. Circa 1835. $2,000-3,000.

The columnar form with several sections is a sign of a late time of origin.

29 Cabinet with one door and rounded side angles, folding panel. Cherry. 80 x 58 x 44 cm. South German, circa 1830. $1,800-2,400.

30 Cabinet with one door, rounded in front, and prismatic sides. Cherry. 82 x 58 x 42 cm. South German, circa 1825. $1,800-2,400.

31 Drum Cabinet, single-door, cylindrical body on octagonal base. Walnut. Height 81, diameter 43 cm. South German, circa 1820. $3,500-4,000.

Interesting and striking forms like these bring higher prices.

32 Cabinet with hidden opening drawer. Cherry with trim set off in black. 94 x 44 x 43 cm. South German, circa 1825. $2,800-3,500.

33 Prie-Dieu with drawer in kneeling bench, side drawer. Setback one-doored cabinet with three small drawers at top and easily tilted panel. Walnut. 99 x 66 x 46 cm. South German, circa 1825. $1,600-2000. *Rare model but not typical of the time.*

Chests of Drawers

34 Pair of chests of drawers. *Two partly gilded Hermes figures flank the two lower drawers and support the slightly projecting top drawer. Original stamped brass hardware. Walnut. South German, Munich, circa 1815. $20,000 and more.*

Despite all their Biedermeier form, these chests of drawers still show clear reminiscences of Empire days. Above all, the added Hermes figures afford a touch of the monumental. Typical Munich furniture from the early times. Matched pieces of furniture are extremely rare and in demand; therefore, they always bring higher prices than comparable individual pieces.

35 Chest of drawers. *Projecting top drawer with printed frieze.*
Cherry, 85.5 x 118 x 57.5 cm.
Munich, probably by Johann Georg Hiltl, circa 1820. $8,000-10,000.

Johann Georg Hiltl showed, for the first time, in 1818-19, furniture that was decorated with the well-known ceramic process of transfer-printing.

34

35

36

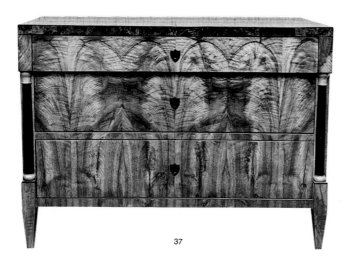

37

38

36 Chest of drawers. *Classic columnar style with gilded bases and capitals. Cherry. 85 x 115.5 x 65 cm.*
South German, circa 1820. $3,750-4,750.

Typical chest of drawers form with clear outlines, projecting top drawer and polished black columns, particularly characteristic of southern and southwestern Germany.

37 Chest of drawers. *Overall veneered panel rimed by two inlayed lines and with striking crotch-grained frieze.*
Walnut, harmonious veneer pattern. 86 x 117 x 58 cm.
South German, circa 1820-25. $4,000-5,000.

In furniture from the Munich area, the top and base forms completely integrated into the outline can be regarded as a regional specialty. The carefully chosen veneer pattern and the well-built, shellac-polished condition justify a higher price.

38 Chest of drawers, *black-painted half-columns.*
Cherry crotch grain veneer. 90 x 128 x 65 cm.
South German, circa 1820-25. $3,800-4,800.

Interesting veneer pattern, in which the usually avoided branch locations were used deliberately to make a lively pattern.

39 Chest of drawers, *three drawers.*
Elm with birch grain. 86 x 123 x 67 cm.
Circa 1820-25. $3,000-4,000.

Elm, unlike the similar cherrywood, is not very much in demand.

40 Chest of drawers *with typical veneer pattern.*
Cherry. 80 x 104 x 55 cm.
Circa 1825. $3,800-4,800.

41 Chest of drawers, *two bowed drawers with a top drawer projecting above them. Carefully selected veneer pattern that unifies the chest of drawers optically.*
Walnut grain. 90 x 125 x 60 cm.
Circa 1820-25. $4,000-5,000.

39

40

41

42

44

43

45

42 Chest of drawers on blocked feet.
Walnut. 89 x 130 x 67 cm.
Circa 1825-30. $3,000-3,500.

43 Chest of drawers, *nicely proportioned, with black-painted columns and projecting top.*
Walnut. 84 x 92 x 45 cm.
South German, circa 1820-25. $3,000-3,500.

44 Chest of drawers *with flanking full columns, their cylindrical bases ending in feet.*
Walnut. Circa 1820-25. $3,500-4,500.

45 Chest of drawers *with projecting bottom drawer, deep middle drawer set off by wedge profile and matching top drawer. Needs restoration.*
Mahogany. 76 x 86 x 54 cm.
North German, Berlin, circa 1820-25. $2,750-3,500.

46

48

47

49

48 Chest of drawers, *four drawers with matching top projecting at the sides. The top drawer features fine ornamental and floral inlays and central shell ornamentation of maple.*
Walnut. 88 x 118 x 60 cm.
North German, circa 1830-35. $3,500-4,000.

47 Chest of drawers *bordered by two black polished and fluted pilasters.*
Cherry. 81 x 106 x 56 cm.
Circa 1825. $3,000-3,800.

48 Chest of drawers. *Two drawers, black polished inset columns with bronze trim.*
Walnut. 78 x 83 x 49 cm.
South German, circa 1825. $3,500-4,500.

Popular chest of drawers form because of its harmonious proportions.

49 Chest of drawers. *Typical South German chest of drawers with simple, unified form. Original brass hardware stamped with figures, lively veneer pattern.*
Walnut grain wood. 86 x 115 x 56 cm.
South German, circa 1820-25. $2,750-3,500.

Salon in Auersperg Castle, Lower Austria, 1818 (above).

Reception room in Windischgrätz Castle, Winternitz, Bohemia, 1830(below).

50 Chest of drawers. *Prismatic three-drawer body with offset top. Needs restoration. Cherry. 82 x 120 x 60 cm. South German, circa 1820. $1,800-2,500.*

51 Chest of drawers, *three drawers, shield-shaped ebonized keyhole design. Walnut. 83 x 121 x 56 cm. South German, circa 1820-25. $2,800-3,500.*

50

51

52

53

54

52 Chest of drawers. *Black painted profiling on the base and top. Ebony keyhole shields.*
Cherry. 82 x 104 x 53 cm.
South German, circa 1820-25. $2,800-3,500.

53 Chest of drawers, *narrow three-drawer body with angled corners.*
Walnut. 84 x 84 x 51 cm.
Circa 1825. $2,800-3,500.

54 Chest of drawers, *narrow body on curved and tapered square feet.*
Walnut. 87 x 86 x 50 cm.
South German, circa 1825. $3,000-3,500.

55

56

55 Chest of drawers. *Three drawers, with projecting base. Cherry.*
North German, circa 1825. $2,000-2,800.

The condition, requiring restoration, determines the relatively low price.
56 Chest of drawers *with slightly projecting one-drawer bottom section. The cut corner angles and the cutout arch on the middle drawer are accented with rootwood inlays.*
Birch. 84 x 107 x 56 cm.
North German, circa 1825. $3,000-4,000.

57 Chest of drawers. *Typical North German chest of drawers with slightly conical basic form; drawers stepped and slightly extended to the sides. The complete profiled edge extends out beyond the top.*
Mahogany. 84 x 93 x 50 cm.
Flensburg, circa 1815-20. $4,000-4,800.

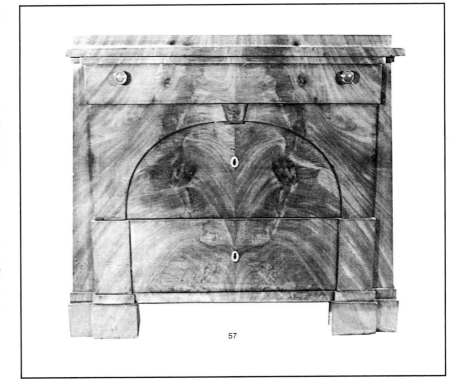

57

58

59

60

58 Chest of drawers, curved bottom board extending into conical feet. Top drawer with framed field of birch surrounded by line.
Mahogany. 63 x 75 x 46 cm.
North German, circa 1825. $2,000-2,800.

59 Chest of drawers Stepped bottom and top drawers extending to the sides.
Birch. 86 x 87 x 48 cm.
North German, circa 1825-30. $1,800-2,200.

60 Chest of drawers. The basic form and the pointed square feet are clear reminders of Louis XVI style. Polished black inlays with inlaid brass ornamental bands.
Cherry. 79 x 97 x 47 cm.
South German, circa 1815-20. $3,500-4,500.

61 Chest of drawers. Two drawers, double frame bands on all sides. Feet and angled corners with ornamentation. Central lyre inlay in maple on the top, colored black.
Cherry. 77 x 114 x 56 cm.
South German, circa 1820. $3,500-4,500.

This chest of drawers has typical, carefully inset, accentuating surface decoration.

62 Chest of drawers. Classic South German Biedermeier chest of drawers with harmoniously grained veneer pattern and warm, pleasant air.
Cherry. 78 x 120 x 59.5 cm.
South German, circa 1820. $3,500-4,000.

When the surfaces of furniture are handled carefully during restoration and their naturally grown patterns can be preserved, they bring higher prices.
The unnecessary treatment of the surfaces of the wood with sandpaper to attain a mirror-smooth surface, and the application of a modern, "easily maintained" artificial finish with an air gun are absolutely false, for they rob any antique furniture of its historical appearance and character.

63 Chest of drawers, two drawers, on tall, tapered square feet.
Walnut. 84 x 99 x 52 cm.
South German, circa 1820-25. $3,000-3,500.

61

62

63

64

65

64 Chest of drawers, *bowed in front. Top encircled by filet band. Diamond-shaped keyhole shields of bone.*
Cherry. 77 x 107 x 53 cm.
South German, circa 1825. $3,000-3,800.

65 Chest of drawers. *The outer contours are united by green-colored birch grain stripes. Base and top surfaces are united without a break. Replaced feet.*
Cherry. 81 x 123 x 60 cm.
Bavarian, circa 1820. $2,000-2,500.

The replaced feet, not in the original style, cause a lower value here.

66 Chest of drawers. *Top and bottom board have brass rims.*
Mahogany. 75 x 63 x 40 cm.
Circa 1820-25. $2,500-3,000.

67 Side stand, *three drawers.*
Cherry. 69 x 35 x 30 cm.
South German, circa 1825. $1,800-2,400.

68 Toilette Chest of drawers. *Two fully three-dimensional carved dolphins flank three semi-circular drawers. Richly appointed top drawer with covered compartments and folding mirror. Top set off with profiled edges.*
Mahogany. 90 x 86.5 x 55 cm.
North German, circa 1825. $4,000-4,800.

Chests of drawers with linen cupboards set into the top, accessible via a folding panel, are a further variant of this type.

66

67

68

69

70

69 High Chest of drawers. *Six drawers, narrow body with two flanking round columns stretching between slightly projecting bottom and top sections.*
Walnut. 140 x 65 x 49 cm.
South German, circa 1820. $6,500-8,000.

The high chest of drawers, also called a chiffoniere today, was often placed baside wall pillars or between windows.

70 High Chest of drawers *with seven drawers.*
Cherry. 155 x 96 x 48 cm.
South German, circa 1820. $6,000-7,500.

71   72   73

71 High Chest of drawers, *double doors with two drawers above them.*
Walnut. 145 x 79 x 41 cm.
South German, circa 1825. $4,750-5,500.

72 High Chest of drawers, *five drawers, with double-line inlays.*
Mahogany. 127 x 55 x 39 cm.
North German, circa 1820-25. $4,500-5,500.

73 High Chest of drawers. *The two middle drawers are combined into one drawer. Stepped top set off by a band of moulding, with projecting gable and built-in drawer, plus ornamental bronze hardware.*
Mahogany. 161 x 90 x 49 cm.
North German, circa 1815-20. $6,800-8,000.

74

75

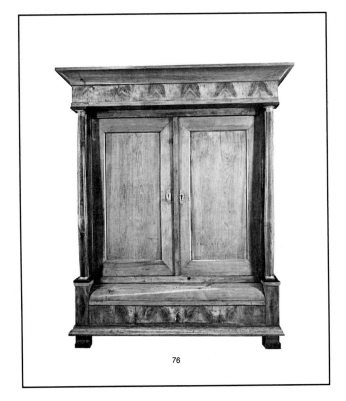

76

Hall Cabinets

74 Hall Cabinet. *The two doors have pointed-arch panels out-side, antique-style friezes and figures inside. Offset top with rootwood added.*
Cherry. 194 x 177 x 64 cm.
South German, circa 1825. $8,000-10,000.

Cabinets, with a height under six feet, stood in the hall or in an anteroom. Clothing and underwear were stored in them.
The shrinkage cracks and resulting damage to the paneled sur-faces of the doors lower the value.

75 Hall Cabinet. *Architectural top design with triangular gable and curved side pieces. Black-framed inlay fields with stylized shell ornamentation. On the doors are framed bands with cen-tral fan rosettes.*
Cherry and maple. 208 x 196.5 x 82 cm.
North German, circa 1825. $9,500-12,000.

Shell ornaments and curved side pieces on a gabled top are signs of North German provenance.

76 Hall Cabinet. *One-drawer bottom section with quarter-round covering. Two full columns beside the two flat paneled doors.*
Cherry. 228 x 197 x 79 cm.
Circa 1825. $7,000-8,000.

77

78

77 Hall Cabinet. *Rounded corners, double-doored body with bottom drawer. Rich decorative inlay with black background, antique-style feminine figures, floral tendrils, flower basket with bird, flower-wreathed archer, filigree rosettes and shell ornaments.*
Oak, maple, and walnut. 230 x 165 x 62 cm.
North German, Hamburg, circa 1830-35. $5,500-7,000.

Typical North German hall cabinet. Despite the splendid inlay work, the height and choice of oak as material determine the modest price.

78 Hall Cabinet *with extending, deeply undercut moulding.*
Cherry. 190 x 159 x 62 cm.
Southwest German, circa 1825. $5000-6000.

79 Hall Cabinet. *Two-drawer base, large pointed-arch panels on the doors. Deeply undercut overhanging top moulding.*
Cherry. 249 x 208 x 83 cm.
Southwest German, circa 1830-35. $4,000-5,500.

Unusual height for a Biedermeier cabinet.

79

80

81

82

83

84

80 Hall Cabinet with doubled base moulding, offset top with moulded band and frontal triangle gable.
Cherry. 198 x 159 x 63 cm.
Circa 1820-25. $4,000-5,000.

81 Hall Cabinet. Black polished decorative profile accenting the schematic structure.
Walnut. 210 x 152 x 55 cm.
South German, circa 1830. $3,000-4,000.

Typical damage on one framed door panel caused by unfavorable climatic conditions lowers the price.

82 Hall Cabinet. Body with rounded edges, two grooved rectangular panels in each door.
Cherry. 200 x 170 x 60 cm.
Circa 1835. $3,800-4,500

83 Hall Cabinet. Projecting scrolled cornice moulding with stylized shell ornamentation in the middle.
Oak. 217 x 167 x 62 cm.
North German, circa 1835. $2,000-2,800.

In this cabinet too, the choice of oak determines the relatively low price.

84 Hall Cabinet. Cut front corners. Nicely flamed veneer pattern.
Cherry. 207 x 165 x 58 cm.
Circa 1825. $3,800-5,000.

Wardrobes

85 Wardrobe. projecting angled moulding all around.
Walnut, massive. 184 x 117 x 56 cm.
South German, circa 1825. $3,800-4,500.

86 Wardrobe, curved in front, flanked by two ribbed full columns. Both doors have round-arch panels. Shield-shaped keyhole covers of mother-of-pearl surrounded by bands of ebony.
Walnut. 182 x 116 x 58 cm.
Central German, circa 1825. $5,200-6,000.

87 Wardrobe. Curved front, flanked by two ribbed columns. Projecting flat top with cornice molding.
Walnut. 193 x 142 x 68 cm.
Central German, circa 1830-35. $5,500-6,200.

88 Wardrobe. The two curved doors have pointed-arch panels with tracery and stylized flowers in Gothic style.
Apple and birch. 173 x 117 x 66 cm.
Circa 1830. $4,000-4,800.

Biedermeier furniture with Gothic-style decorative elements is often misidentified and thus not priced as high as the smooth pieces with veneered surfaces.

85

86

87

88

89

90

91

89 Wardrobe. Double doors with flanking full columns.
Walnut. 184 x 129 x 62 cm. $3,800-4,200.

The veneer pattern, bleached by sunshine, needs restoration.

90 Wardrobe. Smooth board bottom, stepped top with central
drawer. Later hardware.
Mahogany. 230 x 140 x 52 cm.
South German, Württemberg, circa 1815-20. $3,500-4,800.

South German or Württemberg furniture often has an almost
monumental basic form derived from Empire style; here it is
made even stronger by the closed bottom. The conception of the
surfaces, though, shows this wardrobe to be definitely early
Biedermeier furniture, even though the bronze hardware was
added at a later time.

91 Wardrobe. Two wide inlaid fields with doubled pilaster col-
umns covered by rootwood flank the similarly decorated door
frames with round-arch paneling.
Cherry, 180 x 125 x 55 cm.
Circa 1830-35. $9,500-12,000.

92

93

92 Wardrobe, with double doors and warped inlaid fields. Slightly offset top with raylike wave decor and completed by cornice profile.
Walnut. 190 x 145 x 62 cm.
Circa 1830. $4,000-4,800.

93 Wardrobe on straight base with striking double band veneer.
Elm. 199 x 140 x 58 cm.
Central German, circa 1825. $3,00-3,750.

The choice of elm and the condition, which requires restoration, cause the somewhat low price.

94 Wardrobe. Simple body with ribbed corner posts and corresponding stylized scroll feet.
Walnut. 165 x 101 x 47.5 cm.
Circa 1830-35. $3,500-4,000.

94

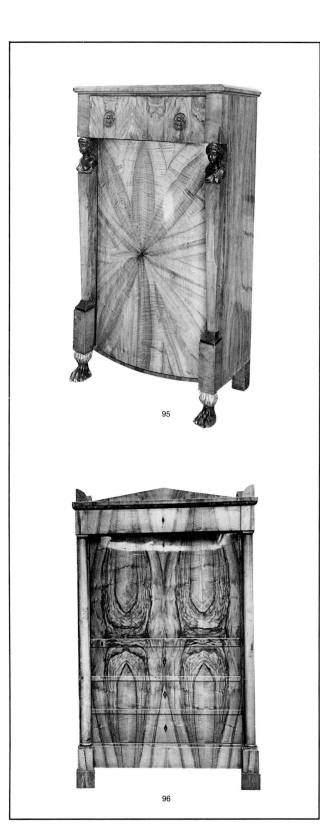

95

96

97

Linen Cupboards

95 Pair of Linen Cupboards *on finely carved, partly gilded paw feet. Two antique-style busts of women, on tapering pedestals and flanking the star-veneered curved door with central bar lock, support the slightly offset, one-drawer top.*
Walnut. 155 x 92 x 49 cm.
Viennese or South German, circa 1815-20. $20,000-25,000.

This decorative but livable pair of cabinets indicates the prevalence of efforts made in the Biedermeier era to bring case furniture for linens and clothing into the living area. That this solution, compelled by the limited available space, was handled successfully by the artisans of the time in terms of form and artistic design, is shown by these masterfully made twin pieces with their splendid veneer pattern.

96 Linen Cupboard, *with one door, front layout in the manner of writing cabinets, lively veneer pattern.*
Walnut crotch grain. 175 x 113 x 59 cm.
Circa 1825. $3,500-4,500.

Another imaginative treatment of a linen cupboard is seen in this piece, which has the traditional layout of a writing cabinet.

97 Linen Cupboard. *Architecturally designed front with flanking columns in typical Corinthian style. The doors are laid out in the manner of writing cabinets.*
Flame-grained birch. 198 x 128 x 75 cm.
Probably from Berlin, circa 1825-30. $3,800-4,500.

98

99

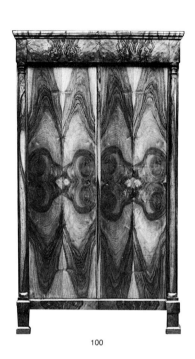

100

101

Characteristic of Berlin style is a strong architecturally designed front facade. Here the columns take on their Classical function as supporting members for the powerful architrave and the dental molding, and thus are not, as otherwise in Biedermeier furniture, exchangeable decorative work (compare the writing cabinet, designed by K. F. Schinkel, at Charlottenburg Castle in Potsdam).

98 Linen Cupboard, one door, with typical writing-cabinet front. The top drawer, including parts of the cornices, and the rounded corners clearly indicate the later phase.
Walnut, 160 x 108 x 55 cm.
South German, circa 1835-40. $2,000-2,500.

99 Linen Cupboard, one door, narrow pillar form.
Cherry. 160 x 82 x 57 cm.
Circa 1830-35. $2,500-3,000.

100 Linen Cupboard. Typical basic form with two doors and harmonized top drawer.
Walnut. 181 x 108 x 53 cm.
Circa 1825-30. $2,800-3,500.

101 Linen Cupboard. Balanced proportions, harmonious veneer pattern.
Wild cherry. 169 x 100 x 51 cm.
South German, circa 1820-25. $2,800-3,000.

The panels are veneered with a lively decorative pattern.

A room at Schönbrunn Castle, drawn by J. B. Höchle, 1818 (above).

A room in the Kinsky Palace in Prague, circa 1820 (below)

102

103

Corner Cupboards

102 Corner Cupboard. *Body with rounded edges, doors with flat panels, drawer in between. Figures and ornamental hardware of bronze.*
Mahogany. 215 x 105 x 60 cm.
Circa 1820-25 $5,000-6,000.

Corner furniture became very popular in the Biedermeier era. It took the stiffness out of corners and offered additional storage space within the limited living space.

103 Corner Cupboard. *Quarter-round shape with wide matching inlay patterns, two doors above and two below.*
Mahogany, 211 x 110 x 71 cm.
Circa 1820-25. $4,500-5,200.

104

105

Writing Cabinets

At the beginning of Classicism, writing cabinets came to prevail over the upright secretaries with slanted writing panels that were so popular in the Baroque era. They show a unified layout with at most three drawers, a folding writing panel above them, often opening to expose a rich "inner life", and a final drawer at the top. In northern Germany in particular, they were often crowned with imaginative top designs, This type of writing cabinet became a generally widespread and popular piece of furniture during the Biedermeier era.

In such standardized types of furiture, formal arrangement, impressive decoration, choice of wood and lavish design of the interior determine the value.

*104 Lyre Secretary. With offset drawer. The lavishly divided secretary interior includes secret drawers. Mahogany.
155 x 123 cm.
German, circa 1830. $40,000-50,000.*

*105 Writing Cabinet. Two black polished full columns flank the three-drawered body with the writing panel above and support the projecting top with its single drawer. Splendid, architecturally designed secretary arrangement with multi-colored landscape painting on the many compartments. A fine Classic frieze on the top drawer.
Walnut.
Weimar, circa 1815-20. $18,000-20,000.*

Harmonious design and precisely detailed, architecturally formed interior with high-quality miniature painting on the compartments enhance the value.

106 Writing Cabinet. *Classic front design with concave, one-drawer top. Finely ornamented drawer handles made of bronze.*
Mahogany. 149 x 94 x 52 cm.
South German, circa 1815. $6,000-8,000.

This South German piece of furniture shows its departure from Empire style by its pointed feet, which make the piece look lighter, and the concave top drawer that makes the piece look less strict and space-consuming.

107 Writing Cabinet *on paw feet. The three-drawer design of the lower part is covered by two doors. The writing panel and doors have shrinkage cracks and need restoration.*
Mahogany. 148 x 97 x 41 cm.
South German, circa 1815-20. $6,000-8,000.

This writing cabinet, like many other South German pieces, clearly shows the standard form of the Empire style that immediately preceded it. The weighty basic form, massive full columns and paw feet emphasize this. The fact that it is nevertheless an early Biedermeier piece is shown by the deliberate design of the front facade and the surface conception, very much in the Biedermeier spirit, without added bronze decorations.

106

107

108   109   110

111

Characteristic form of the Southwest, with a simple, unified form, heavy post feet and black polished flanking columns. The price requires a faultlessly made, shellac-polished condition, as in this example.

109 Writing Cabinet with a simpler interior layout; its condition requires restoration.
Cherry. 152 x 103 x 52 cm.
Southwest German, circa 1820-25 $6000-8,000.

110 Writing Cabinet. Architectural front thoroughly influenced by Empire style, flat gable projecting far out, set off by gilded scrolls covering the top panel; rich bronze hardware.
Mahogany. 184 x 123 x 62 cm.
Berlin, circa 1815. $10,500-14,000.

The design, seemingly put together using individual cubes, identifies this furniture as an early product of the Biedermeier era. The still monumental atmosphere, along with the architecturally designed superstructure, plus the use of lavish bronze decoration, goes back to the influence of Karl Friedrich Schinkel and is typical of much Berlin and Prussian furniture of that time.

111 Writing Cabinet. Clearly recognizable is the typically North German front formation, set off from the body, in connection with a multiple-stepped top and flat gable with front band, as well as recessed panels.
Mahogany, North German, circa 1820. $5,500-7,000.

108 Writing Cabinet. Secretary layout with several drawers, architecturally designed, mirrored middle section.
Walnut, mahogany and apple birch. 145 x 112 x 60 cm.
Southwest German, circa 1825. $7,000-9,000.

112   113   114

112 Writing Cabinet with flanking columns on a stepped base.
Several drawers are inside, with central folded-star inlay.
Mahogany. 165 x 115 x 60 cm.
North German, circa 1825-30. $5,000-6,000.

113 Writing Cabinet. *Body extends upward; bottom drawer with*
semi-circle cut in, top drawer flows into cornices.
Mahogany. 132 x 90 x 51 cm.
North German, circa 1835. $6000-8,000.

The pryamid shape and curved band on the bottom drawer are
characteristic of North German products. The flowing lines of
the top drawer and the cutout silhouettes of the pigeonholes are
indications of an origin after 1830.

114 Writing Cabinet. *Cubic shape with Classic front sectioning*
and many drawers inside.
Mahogany. 142 x 123 x 53 cm.
North German, circa 1820-25. $4500-5,500.

115 Writing Cabinet with black polished grooves in the inlays.
Ash. 174 x 112 x 57 cm.
Central German, circa 1825. $2,800-3,500.

Ash as the chosen wood is not very highly valued today. Ash
was used above all in the central German areas oriented to-
ward Bohemia.

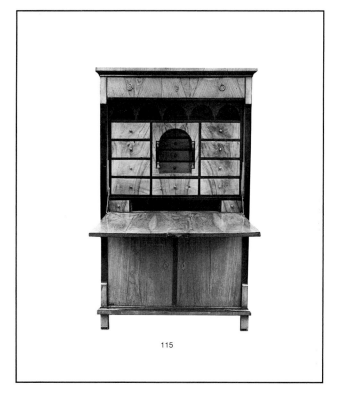

115

116   117   118

119

116 Writing Cabinet with raised top drawer. Frame bands set off in black, and the inlaid figure of a knight on the writing panel.
Cherry. 157 x 94 x 45 cm.
Circa 1820-25. $4,500-5,800.

117 Writing Cabinet. The rounded corners, flowing cornices by the top drawer, and the playful ornamental inlays on the drawers in the secretary indicate a later form here. Rich architecturally shaped and mirrored middle drawer.
Nicely grained walnut. 162 x 110 x 55 cm.
Circa 1835-40. $4,800-6,000.

118 Writing Cabinet. Three-quarter columns support the top moulding with flowing cornice.
Cherry. 157 x 103 x 48 cm.
Circa 1830-35. $4,800-6,000.

119 Writing Cabinet. Rounded corners and front clearly divided by raised mouldings are characteristics of the later period.
Mahogany. 154 x 107 x 51 cm.
Circa 1835-40. $2,750-3,500.

120 Writing Cabinet. Simple box form with flanking full columns and panel completing the pattern. Portico-like addition is set back.
Mahogany. 200 x 113 x 62 cm.
Southwest/Central German, circa 1820-25. $8,000-10,000.

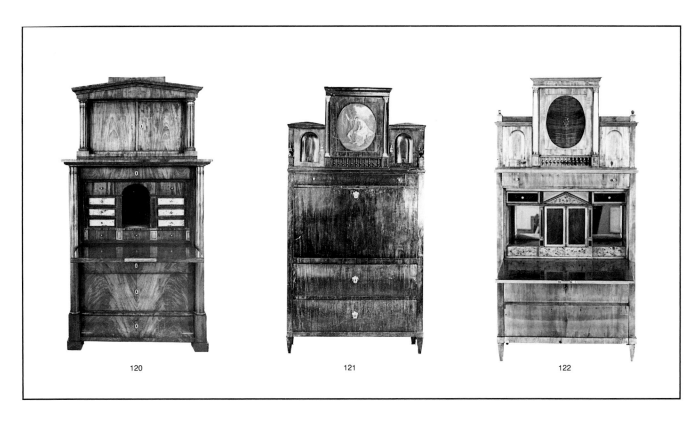

120   121   122

121 Writing Cabinet. *Two drawers, richly furnished secretary section above them, closed by folding writing panel. Over the top drawer is a stepped top. The elegant central section has flanking columns and bottom balustrade. On the door are oval painted pictures with antique-style figures in landscapes. Flat gabled side boxes, each door with a rounded-arch niche. Mahogany. 180 x 90 x 45 cm. North German, circa 1815-20. $10,000-12,000.*

Clearly visible in this typically North German early Biedermeier furniture is the close dependence on the form of the Louis XVI style. Outer unity, straight lines, even surfaces and the light touch accented by the pointed feet show off the actual body of the secretary. These qualities are typical of Louis XVI style but also of British furniture.

122 Writing Cabinet, *here with opened writing panel. Architectural door compartment flanked by back-mirrored pigeonholes with secret mechanism. Top drawer built as lectern. Cherry. 199 x 105 x 48 cm. North German, circa 1815-20. $9,500-11,000.*

The top drawer lowers, when pulled out, to form a sloping writing panel and thus allows short-time writing while standing.

123 Writing Cabinet. *Many drawers and partial mirrors in the secretary, sliding tablet panel in the stepped moulding frieze. Two-door top section with central stagelike, mirrored niche and flanking pilaster caryatids. Mahogany. 171 x 102 x 46 cm. North German, circa 1815-20. $6000-8,000.*

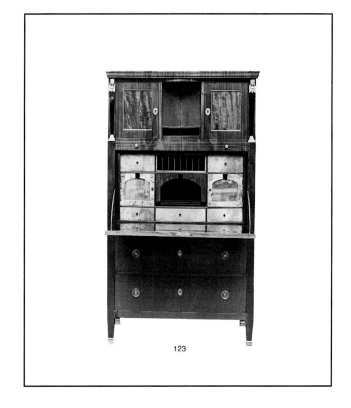

123

124

125

126   127

124 Writing Cabinet. *The upper part has concave side compartment doors and a half-round temple structure in the middle, including round cupola and mirrored back.*
Birch, cherry and walnut.
North German, circa 1820. $6,500-9,000.

125 Writing Cabinet. *Clearly stepped form composed of bodies of different sizes. Case has offset, sectioned front with characteristic plain frames. Stepped top with three doors.*
Mahogany. 215 x 105 x 70 cm.
North German, circa 1820-25. $8,000-10,000.

This writing cabinet's appearance is typical of the north German area.

126 Writing Cabinet *with elegant, Classic-styled secretary inside and correspondingly ornamented band of moulding. Top with drum-shaped side boxes with a door in each and a temple-like middle part. Round-arched niche inset here with columned center and panels decorated with figures.*
Mahogany. 210 x 105 x 46 cm.
North German or Danish, circa 1820-25. $10,000-12,000.

127 Writing Cabinet *with flanking inset columns. Top section with elegant one-door convex middle and side boxes with two concave drawers in each.*
Birch. 200 x 108 x 55 cm.
North German, circa 1825. $6000-8,000.

128 Writing Cabinet. *Multiple-drawer secretary layout: arcades, central compartment with door, inset copperplate engraved decoration and additional sliding writing panel. One-doored box above, divided by pilasters.*
Mahogany. 183 x 96 x 49 cm.
Central German, circa 1825. $6000-8,000.

129 Writing Cabinet. *Typical front offset from the body. Top with flanking quarter-round side boxes and central one-doored and gabled middle section.*
Mahogany. 186 x 112 x 52 cm.
North German, circa 1825. $5,000-6,000.

130 Writing Cabinet. *Top with curved door, designed in the manner of a portico.*
Flamed birch. 199.5 x 103 x 59 cm.
North German, circa 1825. $6000-8,000.

131 Writing Cabinet *with flanking full columns on the secretary and upper portions, as well as the typical plain frames.*
Mahogany. 215 x 110 x 55 cm.
North German, circa 1825-30. $8,000-10,000.

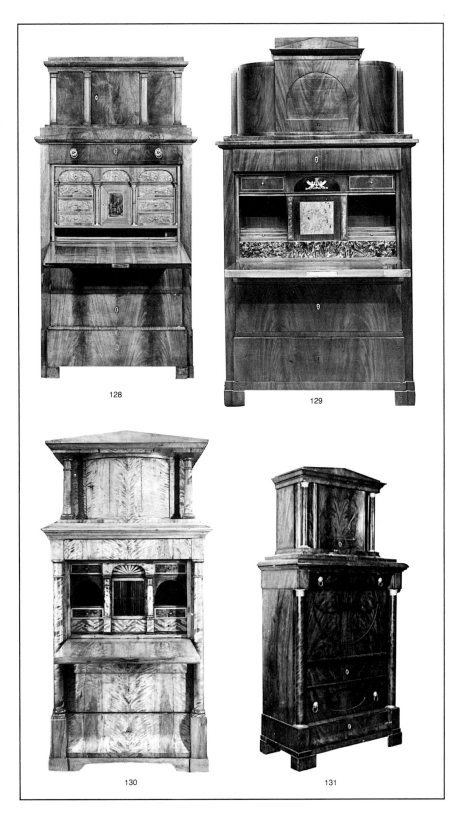

128

129

130

131

132   133   134

135

132 Writing Cabinet. *Offset front, rising in pyramid form to overly high one-doored top section. Nicely arranged writing area with arcade arches between the three rows of drawers.*
Mahogany. 178 x 111 x 50 cm.
Central German, circa 1820-25. $5,500-6,500.

133 Writing Cabinet *with arched, backward-springing bottom drawer, drum-shaped top, volutes projecting at the sides. Plain frames with recessed rectangular and oval panels.*
Mahogany. 212 x 114 x 60 cm.
North German-Prussian, circa 1825. $5,500-6,500.

134 Writing Cabinet. *One-doored semicircular top with stepped roof, set off by gilded egg and dart moulding.*
Birch. 196 x 113 x 56 cm.
Prussian, circa 1820-25. $5,500-6,500.

135 Writing Cabinet. *Simple body with Classic front division on curved pointed feet. Double-doored top section set off by wedge profile, with flat pediment.*
Cherry. 197 x 94 x 50 cm.
Central-Southwest German, circa 1820-25. $5,500-6,500.

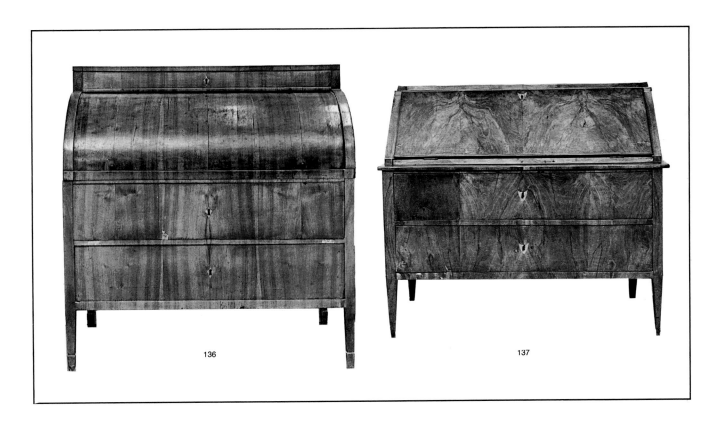

136   137

Desks

136 Desk. *Two-drawered case on tapering square feet. Multiple-drawered secretary layout above with sliding writing panel and cylindrical cover. Drawer at the very top.*
Walnut. 120 x 119 x 66 cm.
South German, circa 1820. $4,000-5,000.

Typical writing furniture of the Louis XVI period, which continued to enjoy a certain popularity in the Biedermeier era.

137 Desk. *Two-drawered, with slightly set-back secretary section with multiple drawers, fall front writing panel, and three-sided rim around top.*
Walnut. 113 x 128 x 61 cm.
South German, circa 1820. $3,500-4,000.

138 Desk, *three-drawers with inset black-polished half-columns. Original ornamentally stamped hardware of sheet brass.*
Cherry. 114 x 120 x 58 cm.
South German, circa 1820-25. $3,000-4,000.

138

139

140

141

142

139 Desk. *Two half-columns flank the three-drawer chest of drawers section. Over it is a sliding writing panel with secretary section and cylindrical cover that open simultaneously, exposing a richly appointed interior. Two stepped top drawers, the upper one rounded. Cherry.*
Southwest Germany, circa 1820. $4,500-5,500.

140 Desk *with typical cylinder closing. Birch. 115 x 112 x 55 cm.*
Southwest German, circa 1820. $4,000-5,200.

141 Desk. *Two drawers optically united by arched band, the upper one with curved, inset panel. Architectural middle section with steel engraving decoration.*
Mahogany. 120 x 110 x 56 cm.
North German, circa 1835-40. $3,000-3,500.

142 Desk. *This desk has an unusually high writing level which suggests it probably was an office model used in a standing position. Elaborate interior layout.*
Oak. 150 x 114 x 52 cm.
Central German-Bohemian, circa 1825. $2,500-3,500.

Writing Chest of drawers

143 Writing Chest of drawers *on stylized feet. Protruding top drawer with folding front and typical, multi-drawered secretary layout. Rosewood inlays surrounding the contours. Walnut, half-grained. 96 x 126 x 61 cm. South German-Bavarian, circa 1830. $4,000-4,800.*

Striking formal design, good choice of wood, eye-catching veneer pattern and perfect condition justify this value.

144 Writing Chest of drawers *with writing panel folded out. Walnut, 93 x 122 x 63 cm. Southwest German, circa 1820-25. $4,000-4,800.*

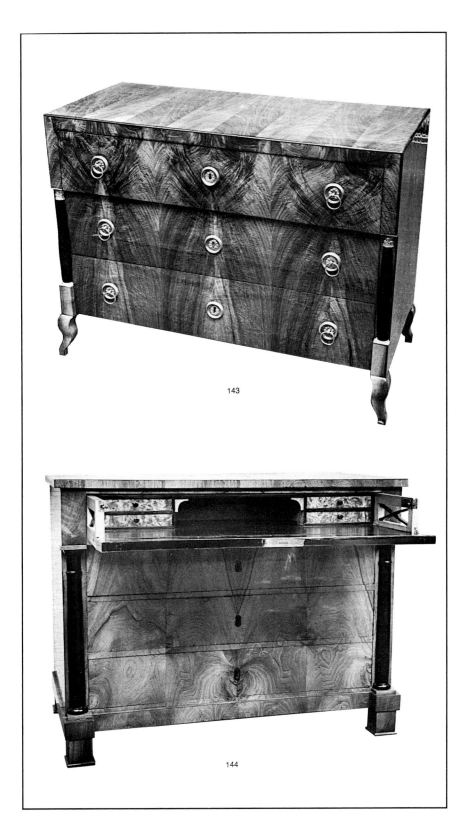

143

144

145

147

146

148

Writing Desks

145 Writing Desk with two small drawers flanking the knee-hole, plus middle drawer. Upright top section set back.
Walnut. 95 x 126 x 74 cm.
Austrian, circa 1820. $4,500-6000.

146 Writing Desk. Writing panel of red leather set into the surface. Central lock on the middle drawer.
Walnut. 78 x 139 x 80 cm.
South German, circa 1820. $4,800-6000.

147 Writing Desk. Table of box design with folding panel, separated in the middle.
Cherry. 80 x 118 x 75 cm.
South German, circa 1820. $4,000-4,800.

148 Secretary. Writing-desk section with setback secretary top, its interior layout concealed by a folding writing panel. Dental-moulding under the top, and a raised moulded box above.
Mahogany. 148 x 145 x 77 cm.
Carlshof Castle in Darmstadt, circa 1820. $4,500-5,500.

This writing desk reflects the re-evaluation of the Empire style that was still utilized, especially in court circles.

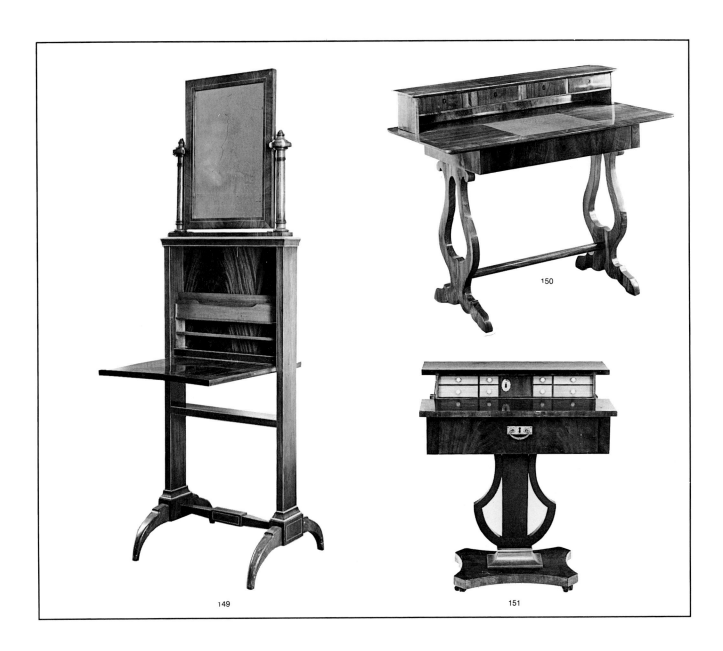

149

150

151

Ladies' Desks

149 Lady's Desk. *Flat vertical secretary section with folding panel. Over it is a rectangular mirror hanging between full columns.*
Mahogany. 169 x 53 x 10 cm.
Prussian-North German, circa 1820. $3,800-4,200.

Simpler design of a form that is usually elaborately decorated and equipped; original small piece of many uses.

150 Lady's Desk. *One-drawer in the skirt that rests on lyre-shaped supports. Overhanging writing surface covered in leather, set-back upright top.*
Walnut. 92 x 112 x 62 cm.
Austrian, circa 1830. $4,000-5,000.

151 Lady's Desk *on flat concave-patterned base. Single lyre-shaped central pedestal supporting the one-drawer table box with raising secretary section above.*
Mahogany. 72 x 74 x 43 cm.
North German, circa 1820-25. $3,000-3,800.

Convertible, multiple-use, small furniture was much-appreciated in the Biedermeier era.

152

154

153

152 Lady's Desk on a base curved inward on the long sides. Table on black polished scroll legs; writing box with tilted writing surface and multiple-drawer interior.
Birch. 90 x 116 x 65 cm.
Circa 1820. $4,500-5,500.

153 Lady's Desk. Between full columns the case is mounted with two drawers, the upper one set up as a writing panel hinged in the front and with a sliding, half-depth top panel.
Walnut. 100 x 103 x 114 cm.
Viennese, probably Josef Danhauser, circa 1820. $5,500-8,000.

Ladies' desks were designed so that they could be set up in open areas.

154 Writing Table. Table with three drawers and slanted desk top.
Walnut. 89 x 82 x 69 cm.
Circa 1825. $1800-2400.

Seating Sets

In determining the values of seating sets, not only do the quality of the formal design and the time of origin play an important role, but so do the firmness of the seat and the condition of the upholstery.

155 a + b Seating Set, consisting of sofa, two bergère armchairs, four side chairs, and a table. Rectangular central columns on stepped bases rounded at the corners. Lyre-shaped bucket seats and chair backs. Star-veneered tabletop.
Walnut.
Vienna, circa 1820. $40,000 and up.

Lively and unconventional, their design represents the essence of Viennese Biedermeier.

Completely preserved original seating sets are extremely rare and sought-after, and therefore are always worth more than the combined prices of the single pieces.

156 Seating Set, consisting of a sofa, two bergère armchairs, two side chairs and table. Ornamental ribbon inlays of maple.
Walnut.
Austrian-Viennese, circa 1835. $12,000-15,000.

The table was probably not originally part of the set, which probably had four side chairs originally, not two. This set probably originated in the transitional years that preceded the later phase; it shows signs of age that need to be restored. The price must therefore be somewhat lower than otherwise.

155a

155b

156

Writing room of Countess Moly Zichy-Ferraris, Vienna, circa 1830. after a painting by Alb. Schindler.

Reception room in a Viennese middle class house, circa 1840, after a lithograph.

Sofas

157 Sofa. *The back, closed on three sides, has deep armrests resting on inset half-columns. Veneer damage.*
Walnut. 95 x 157 x 60 cm.
Viennese, circa 1820-25. $5,200-6,500.

The graceful form and pleasant proportions justify this price despite the ravages of time.

157

158 Sofa. *Rolled seat frame with scrolled armrests on similar, outreaching feet. Plainly rounded back.*
Walnut. 99 x 225 x 70 cm.
South German, circa 1825. $4,000-5,000.

159 Sofa. *Lyre-shaped frame on relief-decorated feet shaped like horns of plenty.*
Cherry. 92 x 195 x 62 cm.
South German, circa 1825-30. $4,500-6,000.

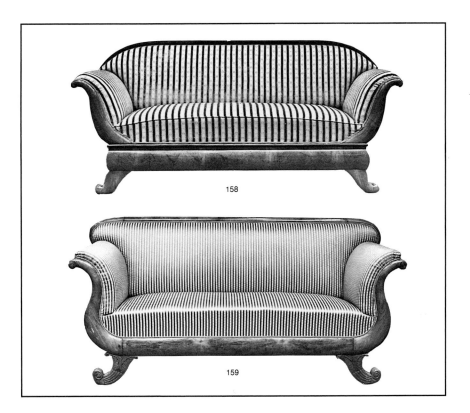

158

159

160

163

161

164

162

165

160 Sofa. Back has flowing, silhouetted pattern, as does the front frame.
Walnut. 103 x 185 x 70 cm.
South German, circa 1835. $2,800-3,500.

The strongly flowing design is typical of the period around or after 1835. Sofa has been reupholstered.

161 Sofa on eight bowed and tapered feet. High back, leaf relief on armrests.
Walnut. 97 x 161 x 69 cm.
South German, circa 1825. $4,000-4,800.

162 Sofa. Bowed back frame with rounded ends. In good condition.
Cherry. 100 x 169 x 60 cm.
South German, circa 1830. $4,000-4,800.

163 Sofa. Open armrests with flat middle sections, flowing back design.
Walnut. 88 x 207 x 73 cm.
South German, circa 1835. $3,000-3,800.

164 Sofa. Curved rear frame with ornamental printed decor. Needs restoration.
Cherry. 96 x 164 x 66 cm.
South German, circa 1820-25. $3,000-4,000.

165 Sofa. Curved arms contine down to form the tapered feet.
Walnut. 80 x 114 x 60 cm.
South German, circa 1820-25. $4,000-5,200.

Charming little "two-seater" in good condition.

166

169

167

170

168

171

166 Sofa. *Curved back with double-scroll crown.*
Walnut. Good condition, with perfect upholstery.
Southwest German, from the Helmstadt estate near Sinsheim,
circa 1830-35. $4,500-5,200.

167 Sofa. *The armrests are designed as horns of plenty. Frame*
bands set off in black.
Cherry. 97 x 210 cm.
Southwest German, circa 1825-30. $4,000-5,000.

168 Sofa. *Rounded back with applied band on top.*
Walnut. 99 x 218 x 71 cm.
Southwest German-Rhenish, circa 1830. $5,200-6,500.

169 Sofa. *The armrests are designed as elegant horns of plenty*
filled with fruit.
Walnut.
Rhenish, circa 1825-30. $5,200-6,500.

170 Sofa. *Relief-carved horn-of-plenty armrests ending in li-*
ons' heads, with bolsters fitting in.
Mahogany. 98 cm high x 218 cm long.
Rhenish-North German, circa 1825-30. $3,500-4,200.

171 Sofa *with wave design at the fronts of armrests.*
Birch. 92 cm high x 228 cm long.
Scandinavian, circa 1835. $2,500-3,500.

172

175

173

176

174

177

172 Sofa. *Straight frame structure with corresponding, clearly raised back.*
Birch. 91 x 201 x 64 cm.
Scandinavian, circa 1830. $2,800-3,200.

173 Sofa. *The armrests have attached half-columns and round bars on top.*
Mahogany. 100 x 209 x 81 cm.
North German, circa 1820-25. $4,500-5,500.

174 Sofa *on scroll feet. Ornamental panel and decorative rosettes on back and armrests.*
Cherry. 94 x 245 x 70 cm.
Circa 1835. $3,800-4,800.

175 Sofa. *The back frame has a raised center.*
Cherry and walnut. 101 x 202 x 70 cm.
Circa 1825-30. $3,500-4,500.

176 Sofa *with upholstery over the back.*
Walnut. 82 x 210 x 82 cm.
Circa 1830. $2,800-3,300.

177 Sofa. *Ornamental reliefs on frame and a flowing back rail.*
Walnut.
Circa 1835. $3,300-4,200.

The relief ornamentation adorning the flat surfaces and the flowing back design reflect the trend for decoration in the later phase, after 1830.

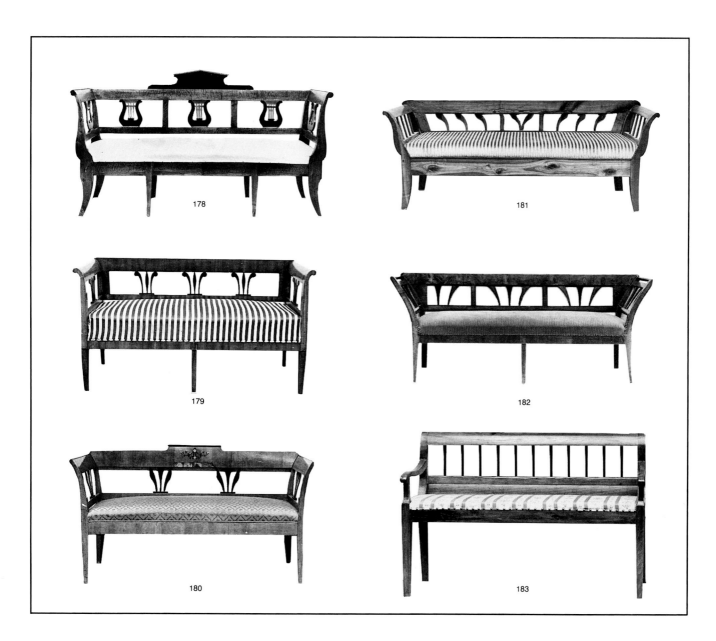

178

181

179

182

180

183

Benches

Unlike sofas, benches have only an upholstered seat, with open arms and back. To be sure, they offer the possibility for the most varied and charming decorations, but do not offer as much comfort as sofas.

178 Bench. *Open back and armrests with polished black lyre supports. Peaked crest on the back rail.*
Pear. 103 x 182 x 55 cm.
South German, circa 1825-30. $4,000-4,800.

179 Bench *with plume-shaped supports.*
Cherry. 82 x 158 x 60 cm.
South German, circa 1820-25. $3,400-4,000.

180 Bench. *Back with central raised crest and floral and figured inlay.*
Cherry. 83 x 148 x 61 cm.
South German, circa 1825. $4,000-4,800.

181 Bench, *round supports for the arms and plumes for the back.*
Cherry. 75 x 200 x 65 cm.
South German, circa 1825-30. $2,400-3,000.

182 Bench *with fan-shaped back and arm supports.*
Cherry. 82 x 205 x 62 cm.
South German, circa 1825. $2,800-3,400.

183 Bench *with straight back and curved armrests.*
Beech. 85 x 127 x 40 cm.
South German, circa 1830. $1,800-2,400.

184

185

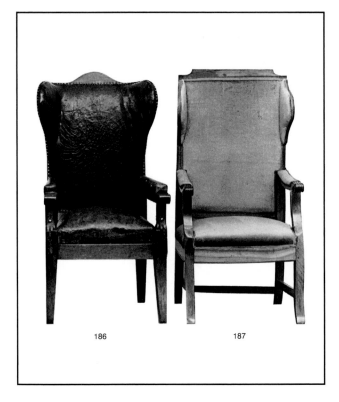

186   187

Wing Chairs

184 Wing Chair *with typical "wings", complete full upholstery.*
Walnut. In good condition. Height 119 cm.
South German, circa 1835. $3,500-4,500.

185 Wing Chair *with upholstered armrests ending in hand*
scrolls.
Cherry.
South German, circa 1825. $3,000-4,000 DM

186 Wing Chair *with adjustable back contrlled by leather belts.*
Stamped leather upholstery.
Oak. Height 129 cm.
Württemberg, circa 1835-40. $1,800-2,200.

187 Wing Chair *with adjustable back controlled by metal bows.*
Cherry.
Circa 1835. $2,700-3,500.

188   189   190

Bergères

Armchairs are called bergères when they are made with full upholstery and closed armrests, and often have a loose seat cushion added to the upholstery.

188 Bergére with curved arm supports and rudimentary scrolls. Walnut. Height 92 cm. Viennese, circa 1820. $3,200-4,500.

Chairs with a semicircular closed back that also serves as arms are also known as Fauteuil de bureau, Fauteuil de cabinet *or* Fauteuil bureau.

189 Bergère with black polished round columns. Walnut. Height 90 cm. Viennese, circa 1820-25. $3,500-4,700.

190 Bergère. High flaring back. Walnut. Height 104 cm. South German, circa 1820-30. $3,500-4,000.

191 Bergère pair. Rounded back with arms ending in dolphin heads. Fruitwood. Height 84 cm. Rhenish, circa 1820-25. $8,500-10,500.

Multiple pieces are always priced more highly than the sum of the individual prices.

191   192

192 Bergère pair. High back with arms ending in dolphin head Mahogany. Height 88.5 cm. Rhenish, circa 1820-25. $6,750-9,000.

193

194

195

Armchairs

193 Armchair with decorative back pattern.
Fruitwood. Height 92 cm.
Circa 1825. $2,500-3,500.

194 Upholstered Armchair pair, *upholstered
back with wide shaped crest rail.*
Walnut, burled wood panel edged in black.
South German, circa 1825-30. $4,400-5,000.

195 Upholstered Armchair pair *with deeply
curved armrests and rounded seat frame.*
Cherry. Height 84 cm.
South German, circa 1825-30. $5,000-5,500.

196 Three Upholstered Armchairs on scrolled feet. Corresponding armrests, ornamental designs set off in black.
Ash. Height 92 cm.
Rhenish, circa 1820-25. $10,500-12,500.

This type of upholstered armchair is characteristic of the late Empire style that was kept alive in the Biedermeier era. It goes back to similar designs used in the Restoration style that prevailed under Louis XVIII in France.

197 Upholstered Armchair. Flaring back and serpentine arms ending in scrolls.
Cherry. Height 99 cm.
Circa 1830-35. $2,000-2,700.

198 Upholstered Armchair pair. Curved top of back and scrolled arms.
Mahogany.
Circa 1820-25. $5,500-6,500.

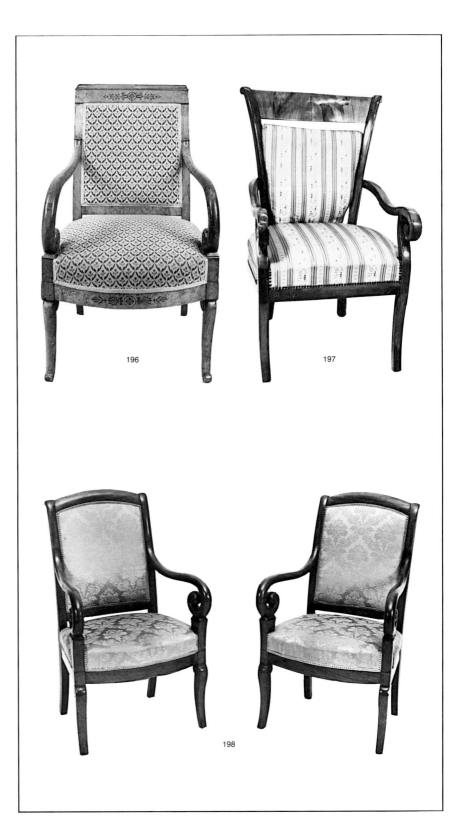

196

197

198

199

200

201

202

203

204

Open Back Armchairs

This type of open back armchair was more popular in the Biedermeier era than the Bergère or the upholstered armchair. With their open backs, they inspired the carpenter to construct them in a manner suitable to the wood. The resulting lightness thus also corresponded to the desired mobility of the chair.

199 Open Back Armchair. *The arms swing up to the stylized back.*
Walnut. Height 90 cm.
Viennese, circa 1815-20. $3,500-4,500.

During the Empire period, Viennese chairs already were characterized by a light air and an imaginative formation of the back. The chairs of the Viennese Biedermeier era were developed directly from them and rank among the most desirable types of chairs.

200 Open Back Armchair. *Wide crest rain lin the back with turned supports rising from a yoke-shaped bar.*
Cherry. Height 91 cm.
South German, circa 1820-25. $3,500-4,500.

Armchairs with the yoke-shaped back pattern are scarce.

201 Open Back Armchair. *Tapering square legs and the back with a lyre design, ribbon inlays with decorative square inlay.*
Cherry. Height 94 cm.
South German, circa 1820. $2,700-3,500.

202 Open Back Armchair. *Frame back with oval openings in the back.*
Cherry. Height 88 cm.
South German, circa 1820-25. $2,700-3,400.

203 Open Back Armchair. *Slightly curved and rounded back with short supports.*
Walnut. Height 88 cm.
South German, circa 1825. $1,800-2,500.

204 Open Back Armchair, *middle bar resembling gathered fabric.*
Walnut. Height 91 cm.
Southwest German, circa 1825. $2,700-3,400.

205 Open Back Armchair, *flat middle bar, shaped crest rail.*
Walnut.
Southwest German, circa 1825-30. $2,500-3,000.

206 Open Back Armchair pair *on baluster legs. Curved back with decorative supports and frame fields.*
Mahogany and apple birch. Height 85 cm.
North German, circa 1830. $4,000-4,700.

Clearly recognizable in these chairs is the relationship in spirit to Britain, seen also in other North German products of this type.

207 Open Back Armchair pair *on clearly curved tapering square legs.*
Mahogany. Height 87 cm.
North German, circa 1825-30. $3,500-4,000.

208 Open Back Armchair. *Deeply curving arms ending in scrolls.*
Mahogany. Height 83 cm.
North German, circa 1825-30. $2,000-2,800.

209 Open Back Armchair *on paw feet. Back with wide shaped crest rail and fan ornamentation with two mirror-image dolphins forming a lyre design.*
Walnut and birch.
North German, circa 1820. $4,000-4,800.

210 Open Back Armchair *with lyre-shaped central splat.*
Elm. Height 109 cm.
North German, circa 1835. $1,500-2,100.

Flowing lines are typical of the later style.

205

206

207

208

209

210

211 Open Back Armchair. *Back with semi-circular opening and top baluster rod. Fabulous beasts set off in gold on black painted background.*
Berlin, probably from a design by Karl Friedrich Schinkel, circa 1830. $3,500-4,000.

212 Open Back Armchair *with plume-shaped back supports.*
Oak and cherry.
Circa 1830. $2,000-2,800.

213 Open Back Armchair *with solid shaped splat.*
Walnut. Height 104 cm.
Circa 1830. $1,800-2,000.

214 Open Back Armchair. *Straight back supports with shaped crest rail.*
Cherry. Height 95 cm.
Circa 1835. $1,800-2,000.

215 Open Back Armchair *with shaped back slats.*
Cherry.
Circa 1835. $1,800-2,000.

216

217

218

219

216 Open Back Armchair. *Cherry. Height 92 cm.*
Circa 1835-40. $1,400-1,800.

217 Open Back Armchair *on tapered shaped legs. Wide curving back.*
Mahogany. Height 83 cm.
Rhenish, circa 1830. $3,000-3,800.

Chairs of this type were used as desk chairs.

218 Open Back Armchair. *The curved arms end in lions' heads.*
Cherry.
Circa 1820-25. $3,000-3,800.

219 Open Back Armchair. *Elegantly shaped rounded back ending in rudimentary scrolls. Frame bands and ornamental inlays on all sides.*
Walnut. Height 86.5 cm.
Circa 1820. $2,700-3,400.

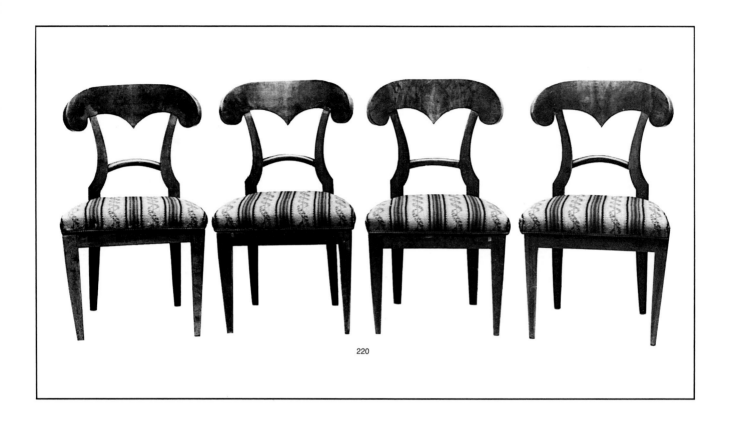

220

221

222

Side Chairs

Side chairs known in Germany as "shovel chairs" were typified by the broad, concave-curved, bowed backs rounded off into scrolls at the sides; their shape reminds one of the shape of a shovel.

220 Set of Four Side Chairs*, in need of restoration.
Walnut. Height 89 cm.
Austrian-South German, circa 1820. $6,000-8,000.*

Complete sets of four chairs or more are in demand and thus always bring more than the sum of the single prices.

221 Set of Four Side Chairs*, in need of restoration.
Walnut.
Austrian-South German, circa 1820. $6,000-8000.*

222 Side Chair *with stylized inlay ornamentation.
Walnut.
North German, circa 1820. $1000-1400.*

The inlay ornamentation on the back is a clue to its North German origin.

223

224

225

223 Pair of Side Chairs, *lyre-shaped central splat, ornamentation with mother-of-pearl inlays. Stamped "AAS" = Master Anders Andersson Strekered.*
Mahogany, height 86 cm.
Sweden-Lindome, circa 1820. $4,000-5,300.

Biedermeier furniture with identifying stamps from the German-speaking area is not known. Masterly quality and faultless condition justify this price.
224 Side Chair *with relief carved dolphins forming a lyre shaped back.*
Walnut. Height 89 cm.
Rhenish, circa 1825. $1,800-2,500.

225 Three Side Chairs.
Walnut. Height 89 cm.
Circa 1820-25. $3,400-4,300.

226 Pair of Side Chairs.
Cherry. Height 90 cm.
Circa 1825. $2,000-3,000.

226

227

227 Set of Four Side Chairs with diamond in-
lays.
Cherry. Height 93 cm.
Circa 1820-25. $6,500-8,000.

228

228 Set of Five Side Chairs.
Walnut. Height 86 cm.
Central German, circa 1825. $10,000-12,000.

Sofa with small table, chair and tabouret, circa 1820 (above).

Table and seating furniture in an Empire room, made by Johann Hertel, Vienna, 1824.

229

230

Ox-head Chairs

Shovel chairs that have a narrow board on the back are also called ox-head chairs.

229 Set of Four Side Chairs *with reed-leaf supports.*
Cherry.
Southwest Germany, circa 1820-25. $6,6500-9,000.

230 Set of Five Side Chairs.
Walnut. Height 94 cm.
South German, circa 1825. $9,500-12,000.

231

231 Set of Four Side Chairs *with black polished columns.*
Mahogany, bleached.
Rhenish, circa 1820. $8,000-10,000.

232 Oxhead Chair.
Cherry.
Southwest German, circa 1820. $1,000-1,250.

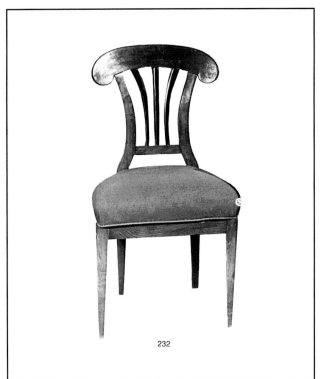

232

233

234

235

236

Reed-Leaf Supports

　　The three-piece decorative supports in the backs of chairs, in their spreading form, resemble a reed plant. This decoration had its origin in British furniture which used three feathers (plumes), as they are shown in the coat of arms of the Prince of Wales.

233 Set of Three Side Chairs and an Armchair.
Cherry. Height 90 cm.
Southwest German, circa 1820-25.　$6,000-8,000.

Table.
Cherry, height 75 cm, diameter 96 cm.
South German, circa 1825. $3,000-4,000.

234 Set of Five Side Chairs.
Cherry.
Southwest German, circa 1825. $4,500-6,000.

235 Pair of Side Chairs.
Cherry. Height 87 cm.
Southwest German, circa 1825. $1,400-2,000.

236 Pair of Side Chairs.
Cherry. Height 86 cm.
South German, circa 1825. $1,500-2000.

237 Three Side Chairs
Beech. Height 90 cm.
Circa 1825-30. $2,400-2,800.

See #281 for table.

238 Set of Six Side Chairs *with baluster rods*
above the crest rail.
Cherry.
South German, circa 1825. $6,500-8,000.

239 Side Chair.
Walnut.
Circa 1825. $550-675.

240 Side Chair.
Walnut. Height 90 cm.
Circa 1825. $525-650.

241 Side Chair.
Walnut. Height 90 cm.
Circa 1820-25. $525-650.

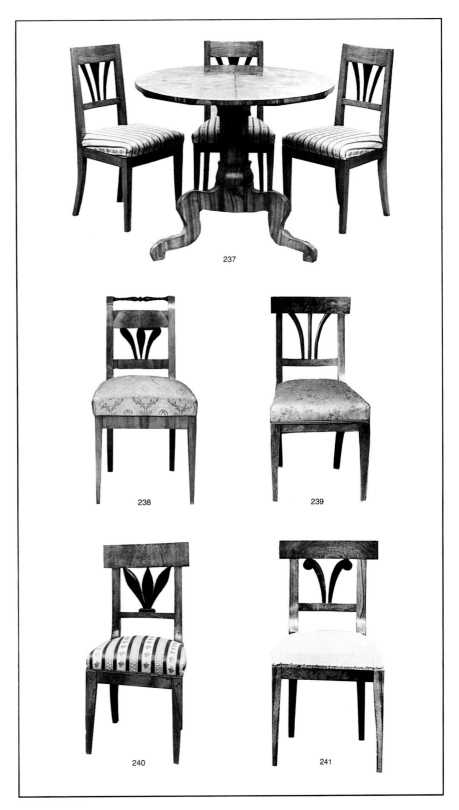

237

238

239

240

241

242   243   244

245   246   247

Various Back Types

242 Set of Four Side Chairs. *Richly decorated back with arch, columns and stylized flower.*
Mahogany.
Vienna, circa 1815. $8,000-10,000.

243 Set of Four Side Chairs *with divided balloon back.*
Walnut. Height 94 cm.
Vienna, circa 1820. $6,000-8,000.

The design of this back resembles that of a balloon, hence the name "balloon back".

244 Set of Four Side Chairs *with eimple balloon back.*
Walnut. Height 92 cm.
Austrian, circa 1820-25. $5,500-6,500.

245 Side Chair. *Back with oval crest rail and crossed arrows behind ornamental central splat.*
Mahogany.
Austrian, circa 1820. $1,200-1,500.

246 Side Chair *in the manner of gondola chairs.*
Walnut. Height 90 cm.
Viennese, circa 1820. $2,000-2,800.

This chair, with its back form, is oriented to the chaises gondoles *that were made in the Empire and Restoration eras.*

247 Desk Chair *with an open back curving around the drum seat like a bergère.*
Walnut. Height 80 cm.
Viennese, circa 1820-25. $2,400-3,000.

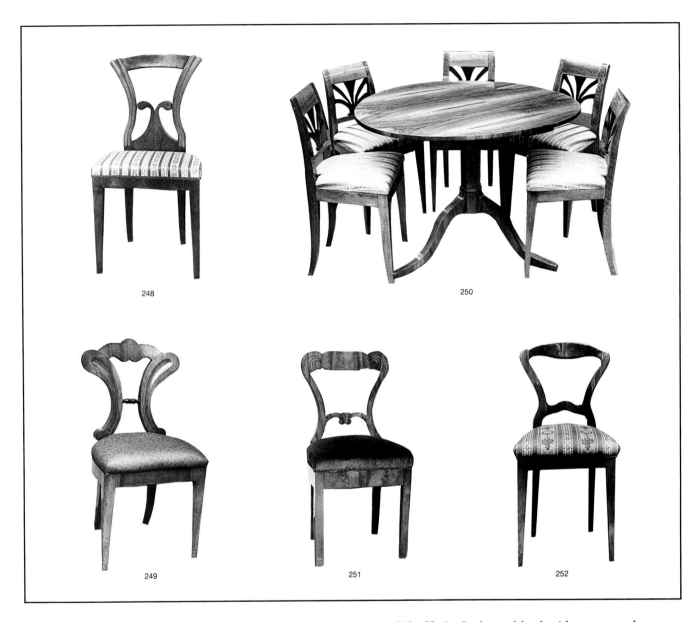

248

250

249

251

252

248 Side Chair with fan-shaped back.
Walnut. Height 91 cm.
Viennese, circa 1825. $525-675.

249 Pair of Side Chairs. *Fan-shaped back with sculptured crest rail and baluster support.*
Walnut. Height 93 cm.
Austrian, circa 1835. $1,200-1,800.

The sculptured crest rail is typical of the later period.

250 Set of Five Side Chairs with black polished fan-shaped back supports. Good, newly upholstered condition.
Southwest German, circa 1825. $6,750-8,675.

See #291 for the table.

251 Side Chair. *Sculptured back with ornamental pattern on the crest rail.*
Walnut. Height 90 cm.
Austrian, circa 1830-35. $525-675.

252 Side Chair with sculptured back.
Cherry. Height 90 cm.
Austrian, circa 1830-35. $400-525.

253   254   255

256

253 Pair of Side Chairs with cut-out floral splat.
Cherry.
South German, circa 1825. $1,800-2,400.

254 Pair of Side Chairs on tapering legs with leaf design on the
back support.
Cherry. Height 86 cm.
South German, curca 1825. $1,800-2,400.

255 Side Chair with cut-out corners in the crest rail and gilded
floral decorations.
Walnut. Height 90 cm.
South German, circa 1820-25. $700-1,000.

256 Pair of Side Chairs. *Lyre-shaped splat with inlaid fan de-
sign.*
Cherry.
South German, circa 1820-25. $2,250-2,700.

See #322 for the table.

257

257 Set of Four Side Chairs *on sabre legs. Shaped crest rail with horn of plenty and flower inlays, decorative pierced slat. Walnut. Height 85 cm.*
Rhenish, circa 1830-35. $4,500-5,250.

See #283 for the table.

258 Set of Four Side Chairs *with solid vase-shaped splat. Walnut. Height 87 cm.*
Rheinsh, circa 1820-25. $4,700-6,000.

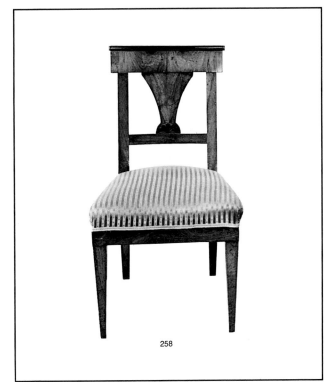

258

259

260

261

262

263

259 Three Side Chairs. *Lyre-shaped back with curved crest rail and carved floral decoration.*
Walnut. Height 88 cm.
Rhenish, circa 1825. $3,750-4,700.

260 Side Chair. *Relief-cut, vase-shaped central splat.*
Cherry.
Rhenish-North German, circa 1825. $1,200-1,800.

261 Pair of Side Chairs *on tapering legs. Central splat carved as fabric gathered in the middle.*
Mahogany. Height 85 cm.
North German, circa 1825. $1,800-2,400.

262 Pair of Side Chairs *with carved open back splat*
Beech. Height 84 cm.
North German, circa 1825. $1,250-1,800.

263 Set of Six Side Chairs. *Side-frame construction with sawed-out slat.*
Mahogany. Height 90 cm.
North German, circa 1835. $3,250-4,700.

In the side-frame construction, the seat is not mounted on the supporting frame as usual, but is set into it. This type of design was especially popular in North Germany.

264 Side Chair with solid vase-shaped splat.
Ash. Height 87 cm.
Central German, circa 1820-25. $1,00-1400.

265 Pair of Side Chairs with flat back panel.
Cherry. Height 92 cm.
Circa 1830. $1,200-1,800.

266 Pair of Side Chairs. *Curved crest rail and*
wide, flat slat.
Mahogany and beech.
Circa 1830. $1,000-1,400.

267 Set of Four Side Chairs. *Two back slats.*
Cherry. Height 87 cm.
Circa 1830. $2,500-3,000.

264

265

266

267

268

269

270

271

Stools

268 Stool. *Rectangular seat on curved tapering legs. Walnut. Height 48 cm. $350-400.*

269 Stool. *Drum seat on curved, splayed tapering legs. Walnut. Height 48 cm. Circa 1825. $475-600.*

270 Pair of Stools. *Cherry. Height 50 cm. Circa 1830. $800-1,000.*

271 Stool. *Rectangular frame with side handles. Walnut. Viennese, circa 1835-40. $800-1,000.*

272

273

272 Footstool in the form of a wide scroll.
Ash.
Viennese, circa 1820. $400-475.

273 Footstool. Rectangular with upholstery of floral petit-point
and pearl embroidery.
Fruitwood. 20 x 36 x 23 cm.
South German, circa 1825. $550-675.

274 Footstool.
Cherry. Height 30 cm.
Circa 1830. $350-400.

274

275

276

277

Tables

275 Table. *Round, star-veneered top with partly ribbed central column on stepped round base.*
Walnut veneer. Height 71 cm, diameter 109 cm.
Viennese, circa 1820. $5,000-6,700.

Striking design with desirable, lively grained veneer. Good condition, polished shellac.

276 Table *on curved base with three feet. Round top with ribbed edge and drum support.*
Top-grained elm. Height 80 cm, diameter 100 cm.
Austrian, circa 1820-25. $3,500-4,000.

Unusual choice of wood plus the tabletop in need of restoration lower the value despite a good design.

277 Table. *Round top on hexagonal column with extending scroll-shaped bows.*
Walnut. Height 81 cm, diameter 95 cm.
Vienna, circa 1820-25. $4,000-4,750.

Two straight braces here protect the tabletop from warping.

278

279   279a

278 Table. *Round top veneered lengthwise, mounted on baluster column.*
Walnut. Height 77 cm, diameter 93 cm.
South German, circa 1820-25. $4,000-4,700.

Perfect condition, polished shellac.

279 Table. *Round, star-veneered top on conforming skirt and hexagonal column ending in a baluster-shaped bottom above the tripod base.*
Cherry. Height 76 cm, diameter 100 cm.
South German, circa 1820. $3,000-3,500.

279a Four Shovel Side Chairs *with black polished decorative support.*
Veneered cherry.
South German, circa 1820. $6,500-9,000.

280 Table. *Hexagonal column tapering upward, with decorative profile.*
Walnut. Height 72 cm, diameter 82 cm.
South German, circa 1825. $3,000-3,500.

280

281

282

283

281 Table. *Oval, star-veneered top with inlaid filet band. Hexagonal central column on three flat, scrolled legs.*
Cherry. 79 x 117 x 93 cm.
South German, circa 1830. $4,500-5,000.

Imaginatively designed piece, ideally constructed. Perfect condition, polished shellac.

282 Table. *Heavy baluster column on scroll-shaped feet.*
Walnut. Height 76 cm, diameter 119 cm.
South German, circa 1825-30. $3,500-4,500.

283 Table. *Hexagonal baluster column on three scroll-shaped legs.*
Walnut. Height 76 cm, diameter 102 cm.
South German, circa 1830. $2500-3,000.

Unrepaired condition and cracked top bring it down to a reasonable price.

284

285

284 Table. *Curved tapering square legs joined by curving X-stretcher.*
Cherry. Height 80 cm, diameter 132 cm.
South German, circa 1830. $2,500-3,000.

Unusually large top for a Biedermeier table.

285 Table *on tapering saber legs joined by black painted stretcher with round plate in the center. The round star-veneered top features fine decorative inlays and a Classic flower vase design in the middle.*
Cherry. Height 78 cm, diameter 89 cm.
South German, circa 1835. $2,500-2,800.

The ornamental inlays on the tabletop show that this table is a product of the later phase. It needs restoration.

286 Table. *Hexagonal baluster column on three-cornered base with scroll decorations, curling up at the ends.*
Walnut. Height 70 cm, diameter 92 cm.
Southwest German, circa 1825-30. $3,500-4,500.

286

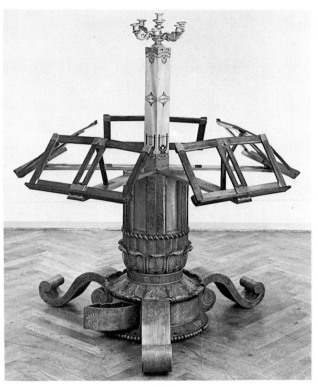

287

287 Convertible Table*. Heavy, elegantly ornamented and inlaid central column with swinging bottom compartments and
extending scroll legs. After the round tabletop is removed, the
table can be converted into music stands for a quintet. The removable square column with candelabra on top is lettered:
"Renotte invenit Expo BXs 1830:. [raised s]
Birch with root grain.
Danish, circa 1830. $12,000-15,000.*

*An imaginative piece of convertible furniture that unites all the
advantages of the Biedermeier cabinetmaker's art. It was shown
in Brussels in 1830 and was used at the premiere of the 1921
Brass Quintet by Carl Nielsen. This is a unique museum-quality
piece.*

288

288 Sofa Table*. Shelf with four curved sides on scroll feet. Round
central column, rectangular top with folding side pieces, one-
drawer in the skirt with bronze ornaments.
Mahogany. 64.5 x 107/152 x 80 cm.
North German, circa 1825. $1,800-2,500.*

*Typical North German sofa table with clear British influences.
Needs restoration.*

Various designs. Viennese School designs, circa 1820-1830.

289

290

291

292

293

289 Table. *Four-cornered base with relief-type scroll feet. Oval top with ribbed support on octagonal baluster column.*
Mahogany. 73 x 119 x 79 cm.
North German, circa 1830. $2,800-3,200.

290 Table. *Triangular column with black painted paw feet on three-legged base with concave sides.*
Cherry. Height 81 cm, diameter 122 cm.
Circa 1820. $3,300-4,000.

291 Table. *Hexagonal column on elegant S-shaped square legs. Round folding top.*
Height 78 cm, diameter 110 cm.
Circa 1825. $2,200-2,800.

The lack of straight moulding caused warping of the tabletop here.

292 Table. *Four black polished scroll legs rise from a rectangular shelf to support the oval top with inlaid border and central circle enclosing a folded star design. The drum skirt has alternating real and imitation drawers.*
Cherry and other woods.
76 x 107 x 93 cm.
Circa 1825. $4,000-5,000.

293 Table *on star-shaped, bowed base. Four saber legs support the drum skirt with four drawers; the oval tabletop is surrounded by an inlaid border.*
74 x 124 x 80 cm.
Circa 1820. $4,000-5,000.

294 Table *on three column legs.*
Cherry.
Circa 1825. $2,500-3,000.

The condition, needing restoration, determines
the value.

295 Table. *Hexagonal baluster column on*
curved tripod legs. Star-veneered top ribbed
on the edge.
Walnut. Height 72 cm, diameter 101 cm.
Circa 1830-35. $2,400-3,200.

296 Table. *Heart-shaped side supports and*
curved feet. One-drawer skirt with overhang-
ing top.
Walnut. 77 x 96 x 62 cm.
Circa 1830-35. $4,000-4,800.

Such tables are often used today as ladies'
writing desks and are in demand for that pur-
pose. Splendid condition, fine workmanship,
polished shellac finish.

297 Table. *Skirt with one-drawer on tapering*
square legs. Top with rim design set off in black.
Walnut. 73 x 94 x 63 cm.
South German, circa 1825. $2,200-2,500.

298 Table. *Skirt with one-drawer supporting*
the overhanging top.
Walnut. 74 x 99 x 66 cm.
South German, circa 1825. $1,000-1,200.

294

295

296

297

298

299

300

301

Console Tables

299 Console Table with Mirror. *A swan flapping its wings on the polished black base supports the semicircular frame carrying the colorful marble top. Over it is a mirror with swans flanking it, a recessed semicircle with bronze decorations above the mirror, and a flat gable at the top.*

Console tables with mirrors no longer enjoyed popularity in the Biedermeier era as they had in earlier times, and thus could only rarely be found in representative room furnishings.

300 Console Table with Mirror. *One-drawer skirt with white marble top, scroll legs at the front. Mirrored back wall, base cut in at the front. Mirror flanked by half-columns; flat top panel and ornamental gable decorated with facing scroll designs.*
Mahogany. 200 x 86 x 43 cm.
North German, circa 1830-35. $3,500-4,500.

301 Pair of Consoles with Mirrors. *Rounded one-drawer skirt over lower back wall decorated with a flower vase design. Rich inlay of flowers and figures on the mirror frames, with stepped top. Antique-style reverse paintings on glass in the upper panels.*
Mahogany and maple. 262 x 70.5 x 38 cm.
North German, circa 1830. $8,000-10,500.

Rare as pairs, and hard to place because of their height.

302

303

302 Console Table. *A black sphinx with remains of old gilding supports the semi-circular skirt and conforming top. Cherry. 87 x 123 x 61 cm. Viennese, circa 1815. $4,000-5,000.*

303 Console Table. *Recatngular table with stretcher shelf and carved "drapery" added in the front. Mahogany. 80 x 170 x 54 cm. North German, circa 1825. $1,800-2,400.*

304

306

305

307

Folding Tables

304 Folding Table with semi-circular skirt on tapering square legs. The back leg folds out to support the folding top which then becomes round.
Cherry. Height 75 cm, diameter 95 cm.
Circa 1825. $2,000-2,500.

This design, particularly popular in Britain, fulfilled the requirements for functionality and mobility in the Biedermeier era. The tabletop is slightly warped.

305 Folding Table.
Birch. Height 75 cm, diameter 70 cm.
Circa 1825. $1,800-2,400.

306 Card Table. Turning and folding felt-covered playing surface on taapered square legs.
Walnut. 78 x 85 x 42.5/85 cm.
Circa 1825. $1,500-2,000.

307 Card Table. One-door bottom decorated with brickwork pattern on rectangular base. A short column supports the canted skirt and turning and folding, felt-covered top.
Ash. 80 x 95 x 47/94 cm.
Circa 1825. $1,800-2,500.

Imaginative variant for a card table.

308

310

309

311

Occasional Tables

308 Occasional Table *on triangular base with convex sides. Scroll-shaped legs and short hexagonal column support the round top with drum frame.*
Cherry. Height 78 cm, diameter 63 cm.
South German, circa 1820-25. $3,000-3,800.

309 Occasional Table *on saber legs with round central shelf. Three-drawer drum frame with round top.*
Cherry, partly painted black. Height 75 cm, diameter 60 cm.
South German, circa 1820-25. $3,000-3,500.

Saber legs feature a curved shape reminiscent of a saber blade.

310 Occasional Table *on saber legs with a shelf in between. One drawer in the skirt and an overhanging top.*
Cherry. 79 x 63 x 48 cm.
South German, circa 1820-25. $2,500-3,200.

311 Occasional Table *on saber legs with triangular base. Round support with overhanging top.*
Cherry, partly painted black. Height 76 cm, diameter 50 cm.
South German, circa 1820-25. $2,100-2,800.

312

312a

313

314

312 Occasional Table, *round, on flaring square legs with a central shelf.*
Walnut top. Height 76 cm, diameter 46 cm.
South German, circa 1820-25. $2,500-2,800.

Popular small furniture with harmonious veneer pattern.

312a Armchair. *Bowed back with raised crest rail and central lyre.*
Cherry.
South German, circa 1820-25. $2,400-3,000.

313 Occasional Table *on four-footed base with concave sides. Skirt with floral embroidery inset on three sides resting on central baluster column.*
Cherry. 80 x 58 x 69 cm.
South German, circa 1825. $2,500-3,000.

Lovely inclusion of needlework in a piece of furniture. Needs restoration.

314 Occasional Table. *Skirt with two drawers and rounded corners, on lyre-shaped side legs. Bowed feet joined by a stretcher.*
Walnut. 60 x 61 x 44 cm.
South German, circa 1830. $2,000-2,500.

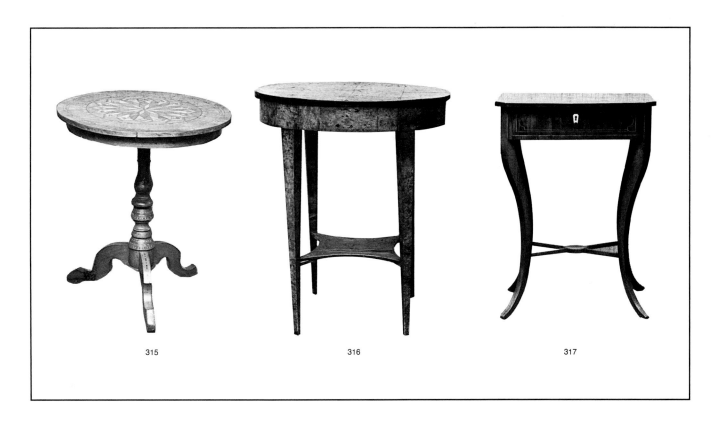

315   316   317

315 **Occasional Table**. *Turned column on scrolled tripod base.*
Round top with fine star and band inlays.
Walnut and other woods. Height 70 cm, diameter 60 cm.
South German, circa 1840. $1,800-2,200.

The turned column, scrolled feet and rich inlays seen here are
signs of the later period of origin.

316 **Occasional Table** *with bottom shelf curved on four sides,*
oval skirt with one drawer.
Root-grained birch. 75 x 60 x 41 cm.
Southwest German, formerly at Bruchsal Castle, circa 1820-
25. $2,500-3,200.

317 **Occasional Table** *on saber legs with crossing stretchers.*
One-drawer in the skirt, top with cut corners.
Mahogany with ribbon inlays of maple. 75 x 56 x 42 c,
North German, circa 1820-25. $2,000-2,500.

318 **Occasional Table** *on curved legs with turned stretcher. Skirt*
with one drawer and rounded corners, ribbed edge to the top.
Walnut.
Circa 1835. $2,000-2,400.

318

319

320

321

322

323

324

319 Occasional Table. One-drawer in the skirt with overhanging top on S-shaped tapering square legs.
Walnut. 76 x 69 x 41 cm.
Circa 1830. $1,200-1,600.

320 Occasional Table. One-drawer in the skirt with overhanging top on tapering square legs. *Walnut.*
Circa 1825. $1,000-1,500.

321 Guéridon on saber legs with triangular shelf between them. Drum skirt with overhanging top and inset marble plate.
Mahogany and walnut with ornamental brass inlays. Height 74 cm, diameter 38 cm.
Viennese, circa 1820. $2,100-2,500.
Guéridons were mainly used to hold candles and knick-knacks, as well as for emptying pockets.

322 Guéridon. Flareded square legs with a round shelf and triangular base.
Cherry. Height 75 cm, diameter 36 cm.
Circa 1820-25. $2,100-2,600.

The turned spindle above and below the shelf was probably added later.

323 Guéridon on scroll legs with two sculptured shelves. Drum skirt topped by a marble plate.
Cherry. Height 87 cm, diameter 35 cm.
South German, circa 1830. $2,100-2,600.

324 Plant Stand on saber legs with intermediate round shelf. Round skirt with inset flower basin.
Cherry. Height 72 cm, diameter 51 cm.
Circa 1820-25. $2,000-2,500.

A zinc or brass basin was set into the tabletop depression, and flowers were planted directly in it.

Sewing Tables

325 Globe Table on triangular base with relief decorations. Three bowed legs with lions' heads and paw feet support the folding, richly appointed globular interior with ornamental band and attached ornament.
Maple, black polished and painted. The carved parts are colored green and gold. Damaged. Viennese, circa 1825. over $30,000.

Owned by the Bavarian National Museum, Munich.

Globe tables rightfully rank among the most desirable small furniture of the Biedermeier era, justifying whatever prices the customer is willing to pay.

326 Sewing Table. *Hemispherical body with richly inlaid decorations and folding tabletop. Flaring tapered legs ending in rams' heads; upholstered footrest on the shelf.*
Maple and rootgrain. Height 72 cm, diameter 46 cm.
Viennese, circa 1825. $12,000-16,000.

Hemispherical sewing tables are rare and sought-after collectors' items in the upper price ranges.

327 Sewing Table *shown with top opened. Cherry. Height 77 cm, diameter 49 cm. South German, circa 1825. $12,000-16,000.*

The hemispherical sewing table offered storage space for favorite pieces of handiwork, reached by removing the interior compartment rack.

328 Sewing Table. *Drum-shaped body with rich interior arrangement. Colored star intarsia on the lid.*
Cherry. Height 74 cm, diameter 50 cm.
Southwest German, circa 1825. $6,000-8,000.

325

326

327

328

329   330   331

332   333

329 Sewing Table *on flared legs ending with paw feet. Triangular shelf in between. Built-in clockwork music box is signed "David Deting, Cassel".*
Mahogany, height 80 cm, diameter 45 cm.
Kassel, circa 1820-25. $12,000-16,000.

330 Sewing Table, *oval, with built-in drawer.*
Walnut. 75 x 53 x 38.5 cm.
South German, circa 1820-25. $2,200-2,800.

331 Sewing Table *with four-drawers in the skirt and brass knobs.*
Walnut with birdseye maple. Height 77 cm, diameter 52.5 cm.
North German, circa 1820-25. $2,600-3,200.

In perfect condition it would be more expensive.

332 Sewing Table *on saber legs joined in the middle and with a star-inlay on the base. Skirt with two front drawers, one above the other.*
Mahogany.
North German, circa 1820-25. $2,600-3,300.

Veneer breakage lowers the value here.

333 Sewing Table *with opened top.*
Mahogany with stringing inlays of maple. 73 x 59 x 39 cm.
North German, circa 1825. $2800-3,200.

The "strings" of the lyres are missing.

334 Sewing Table. The rectangular top overhangs a concave
drawer and hanging cloth bag, all restong on S-curved braces.
Mahogany with inlays of maple. Veneer damage.
75.5 x 54 x 39 cm.
North German, circa 1825. $2,500-3,200

Striking, spirited design that creates an air of lightness.

335 Sewing Table, oval, with top opened.
Mahogany with birch rootgrain interior. 74 x 56 x 43 cm.
North German, circa 1825-30. $2,400-2,800.

336 Sewing Table. Hinged top with figure inlay, showing the
allegory of the winds.
Mahogany with frame-line inlays of maple. 75 x 53 x 41 cm.
North German, circa 1825. $2,000-2,500.

337 Sewing Table with oval top and one-drawer in the skirt,
resting on saber legs with small plate between the stretchers.
Cherry. Needs restoration. 75 x 59 x 43 cm.
Circa 1825. $2,500-2,700.

338 Sewing Table. Oval base concave on the long sides. Two
round columns hold the oval skirt with single drawer and overhanging top.
Mahogany. 77 x 68 x 47 cm.
Circa 1825. $2,700-3,200.

339

340

341

342

343

339 Sewing Table. *Two black polished lyres on a base containing a drawer support the removable sewing chest with hinged lid and side handles. Rich interior detail, decorated with allegorical figures in transfer-printing. Rootgrain, 82 x 58 x 47 cm. Circa 1825. $3,000-3,800.*

Furniture that includes the lyre as a decorative or constructive element is desirable and therefore often expensive. But it is well to take a closer look to see if any factors may lower the value.

340 Sewing Table. *Lyre-shaped side legs with scroll feet support the box with rounded corners and two drawers. Walnut, partly painted black. 78 x 63 x 47 cm. Circa 1830-35. $2,500-3,000.*

341 Sewing Table, *with two drawers and hexagonal column on tripod base with scroll feet. Birch, 80 x 48 x 40 cm. Circa 1830-35. $1,800-2,000.*

342 Sewing Table, *with one drawer, two round columns and stretcher on scrolled feet. Walnut, 77 x 62 x 41 cm. Circa 1830. $2,100-2,400.*

343 Bobbin Stand. *Turned column on round base. One drawer in the skirt with upholstered pin-cushion on top. Walnut. Height 83 cm, diameter 36 cm. South German, circa 1835-40. $1,200-1,800.*

Nightstands

344 Nightstand. *Two round columns with gilded capitals and corresponding bases flank the one-doored body. Projecting top with drawer.*
Walnut. 86 x 46 x 37 cm.
Circa 1825. $1,900-2,300.

345 Nightstand *with black polished pilasters and framed top.*
Cherry. 79 x 35 x 32 cm.
South German, circa 1825. $1,400-1,900.

346 Nightstand. *Front divided between lower compartment with door and upper one with sliding cover, with drawer at top.*
Walnut. 78 x 35 x 30 cm.
Circa 1825-30. $1,400-1,700.

347 Nightstand *with sliding cover on central compartment, false drawer over it and top with raised edge.*
Mahogany. 71 x 35 x 34 cm.
Circa 1825. $1,400-1,700.

348 Sewing Table *with door and drawer above it.*
Walnut. 82 x 42 x 36 cm. $1.400-1,800.

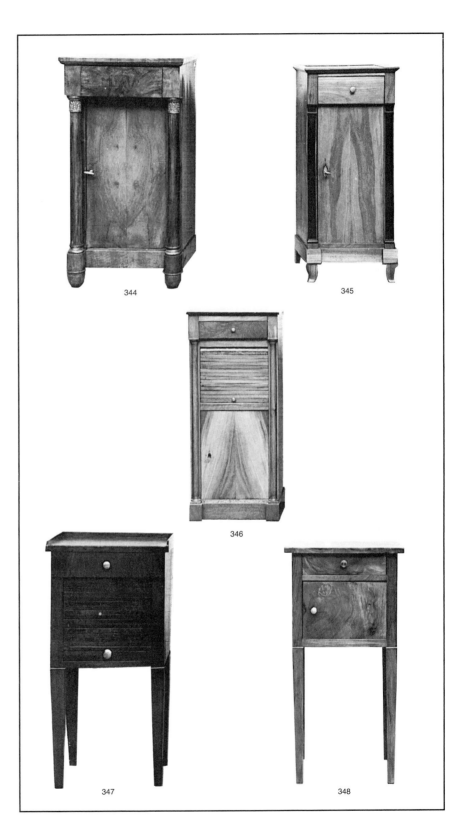

344

345

346

347

348

349

Chests

Toward the end of the eighteenth century, a clearly recognizable regional type of chest with characteristic features had developed in the area around Marburg. It enjoyed a great deal of popularity in the Biedermeier era.

The frequently occurring use of finch figures gave rise to the name of "finch chest".

349 Marburg Finch Chest. *Dovetailed board body with bottom drawers and flanking baluster columns. Inlaid panels on all sides, with that on the top having the typical portrayals of finches on rose branches, and animal figures on the front.*
Oak and other woods. 77 x 114 x 68 cm.
Hessian-Marburg, circa 1830-40. $4,800-6,000.

350

350 Marburg Chest *on straight base including drawers at the sides. Typical rich inlays with figures and decorative bands. Marked "Martha Hornmann in Ebsdorf 1782".*
Cherry and other woods. 72 x 149 x 60 cm.
Hessian-Marburg, circa 1830. $6,500-10,000.

The date 1782 is presumably the owner's year of birth, since the chest is obviously a product of the later Biedermeier era.

Showcases

351 Showcase. *Slightly inset stripes, augmented by gilded caryatids in the upper third, supporting the slightly projecting top, decorated with gilded molding. Glazed doors, the oval field decorated with wheel-spoke braces. Walnut, half and top grain, partly polished black.*
174 x 98 x 52 cm.
Viennese, circa 1815. $10,000-14,000.

Typical imaginative Viennese product of the early period. Efforts to make the glazed surface optically complete by the use of spokes to achieve the desired effect is clearly recognizable.

352 Showcase. *Double-doored body, flanked by round columns. Spoked braces on front glazing.*
Walnut. 204 x 140 x 64 cm.
Viennese, circa 1820. $8,000-10,000.

353 Showcase. *Glazed frame doors with lyre-shaped braces, flanked by black polished round columns. Projecting top with drawer built in. Walnut. 150 x 72 x 41 cm.*
Viennese-South German, circa 1820. $6,500-8,500.

354 Showcase. *The two doors with square panels and brass fittings in their lower thirds; above are glazed panels with crossed arrow braces. Stepped top with projecting flat gable. Mahogany. 164 x 103 x 33 cm.*
Viennese-Central German, circa 1820. $8,000-1,500.

351   352

353   354

355

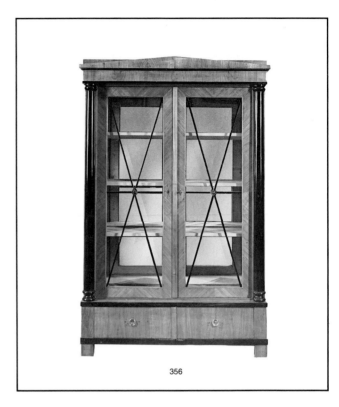

356

357

355 Showcase with framed doors, two-thirds glazed with arrow braces, flanked by black polished round columns.
Cherry. 181 x 118 x 53 cm.
South German, circa 1820-25. $6,000-8,000.

356 Showcase with double drawers in slightly projecting bottom part. Two black polished round columns flank the double glazed doors with crossed-arrow braces. Original mirror on the back wall. Projecting gabled top.
Cherry. 187 x 124 x 46 cm.
South German, circa 1820-25. $8,000-10,000.

The original rear wall in good condition raises the value.

357 Showcase. The double doors with Gothic-style, pointed-arch braces, flanked by polished pilasters. Similar central moulding, with gabled top.
Cherry. 238 x 157 x 42 cm.
South German, circa 1820-25. $6,000-7,500.

The low value results from the height, unfavorable for present-day living conditions.

358

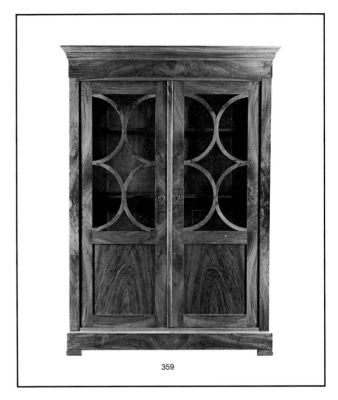

359

358 Showcase with Gothic-style tracery braces, damaged.
Cherry. 175 x 115 x 37 cm.
South German, circa 1825. $4,000-5,000.

359 Showcase with facing semi-circular decorative braces.
Walnut. 195 x 140 x 52 cm.
South German, circa 1825. $4,000-5,000.

Completions required by restoration were taken into consideration in the value.

360 Showcase. High stepped base with a drawer. Double-doored body, glazed on three sides.
Cherry. 195 x 188 x 51 cm.
South German, circa 1820-25. $4,500-5,500.

The side walls of the body were often glazed too, in order to create better lighting conditions for the objects to be displayed. Showcases without side glazing have lower values.

360

Various designs, Viennese School drawings, circa 1820-35.

361

362

361 Showcase (bookcase) with glazed framed doors and beveled corners.
Cherry, partly painted black. 192 x 126 x 53 cm.
South German, circa 1835. $4,700-5,300.

362 Showcase. *Two columns over corners flank the double-doored, front-glazed body with slightly projecting, arched false drawer. Multiple-stepped top with curved drawers and flat gable.*
Birch, partly painted black. 178 x 112 x 51 cm.
North German, circa 1835. $4,000-5,400.

Typically North German furniture with gateway arch in bottom section and multiple-stepped top with drawers.

363

364

365

363 Showcase with two arch-patterned glazed doors. Dental moulding at the top, gabled in front.
Mahogany. 174 x 100 x 33 cm.
North German, circa 1825. $4,000-4,800.

364 Showcase. Case with rounded corners, glass panels in the cross-braced doors and stepped top.
Cherry. 180 x 105 x 45 cm.
North-Central German, circa 1835. $4,800-5,400.

The rounded corners and flowing cornices on the profiled top are marks of the later phase. All the same, cherry furniture is in demand and thus has a higher value.

365 Bookcase Set with corner section and two adjoining cases. Chest section with flat panels in framed doors, plus drawers. Slightly inset upper sections, glazed in front. Brass ornaments on top.
Mahogany. Height 250 cm, length per side 170 cm.
North German, circa 1830. $25,000 and up

A rare and sought-after piece that could bring a much higher price in flawless condition.

366 Showcase. *Two round columns flank the double-doored body glazed in front, on a slightly projecting bottom section with one drawer. Stepped top with flat gable.*
Mahogany with maple frame inlays. 172 x 120 x 50 cm.
North German-Berlin, circa 1830. $4,500-6,000.

367 Showcase. *Two inset round columns flank the half-glazed, ornamented doors. Projecting top with overhanging flat gable.*
Cherry. 180 x 115 x 43 cm.
Central German, circa 1825. $4,500-6,000.

368 Pair of Bookcases *on gilded paw feet. Two half-round columns flank the body, which is open in front. Cropped top profile with moulding.*
Mahogany. 190 x 86 x 43 cm.
Berlin, circa 1815-20. $12,000-16,000.

Unusual pieces with powerful, striking Empire-influenced front aspect typical of Berlin.

366

367

368

369

370

371

372

373

374

369 Showcase. *Two framed doors with oval stiff braces, flanked by figured pilasters.*
Cherry, partly painted black. 174 x 116 x 51 cm.
Central German, circa 1825. $4,300-5,300.

The condition, needing restoration, causes the correspondingly low price.

370 Showcase *with columns set above corners and two half-glazed frame doors with ornamental braces. Offset top moulding.*
Oak. 184 x 121 x 53 cm.
Central German, circa 1825. $2,350-3,000.

The choice of oak is unusual here, as it is not highly regarded for Biedermeier furniture, hence the low value.

371 Showcase. *Body with one door, glazed on three sides, with etagère design.*
Cherry. 157 x 113 x 46 cm.
Circa 1840. $4,300-5,300.

The etagère pattern is an indication of a late date of origin.

372 Showcase. *Tall tapering square legs support two glazed doors and a sliding tambour cover.*
Walnut. 130 x 83 x 41 cm.
South German, circa 1825-30. $4,600-5,500.

The sliding tambout cover on a showcase is very rare.

373 Showcase. *Hexagonal body with door and glazing on five sides. Filet band inlaid around the top.*
Walnut and rootgrain. 161 x 80 x 55 cm.
Circa 1825. $4,500-5,400.

The back wall and the two rear angles were probably mirrored originally.

Servante

374 Servante. *Three columns with round shelves and corresponding stepped top on a one-door drum chest.*
Mahogany with bronze hardware on base and capitals. Height 198 cm, diameter 48 cm.
Viennese, circa 1815-20. $8,000-10,000.

A rare piece, made for holding food and dishes short-term.

Corner Cabinets

375 Corner Cabinet. *Rounded in front, flanked by polished black pilasters. Double-doored lower section, with a row of three drawers and sliding panel. Upper part glazed in front, with two doors and offset top profile with wedge corners.*
Cherry. 204 x 107 x 70 cm.
South German, circa 1835. $6,500-8,500.

376 Corner Cabinet *with flanking polished black half-columns. Bowed double-doored lower section, and slightly inset upper part with four doors, the upper two glazed.*
Spruce. 199 x 103 x 70 cm.
South German, circa 1835. $3,500-4,000.

The unusual choice of wood causes the low price.

377 Corner Cabinet *on bronze paw feet. Prismatic body with two glazed, framed doors.*
Cherry. 210 x 95 x 52 cm.
South German, circa 1820. $5,800-4,200.

378 Corner Cabinet. *Double-doored lower part with sliding panel worked into the moulding. Upper part with two drawers and glazed framed doors.*
Cherry. 230 x 112 x 63 cm.
South German, circa 1830. $3,500-4,000.

379 Corner Cabinet. *Lower part with glazed, framed doors. Inset tapered open storage space, upper part built similarly to bottom.*
Walnut. 192 x 93 x 53 cm.
South German. $3,500-4,000.

380 Corner Cabinet. *Two-part body, rounded in front, with one-door lower part and slightly inset upper part with glazed framed doors. Top with gable blind.*
Pyramid mahogany on veneered oak. Height 207 cm.
North German, circa 1820. $6,500-8,500.

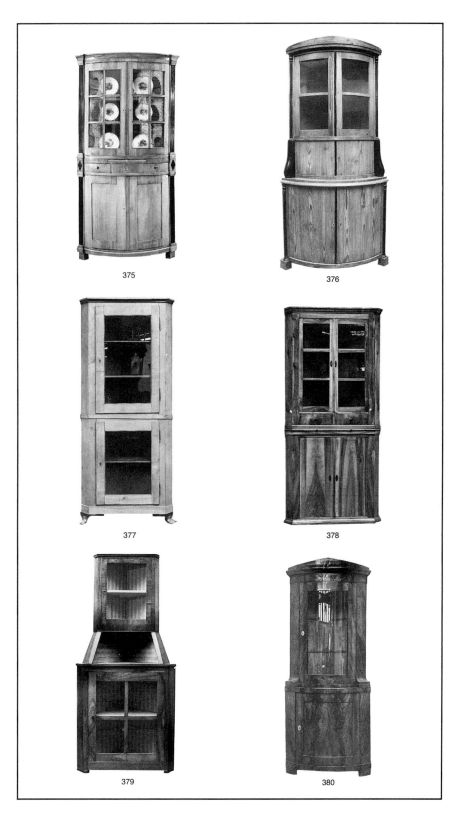

375

376

377

378

379

380

381   382   383

384

381 Corner Cabinet, *one door, rounded upper body set back. Oak with black painted contour border. Height 220 cm. Side depth 75 cm.*
North German, circa 1820. $5,000-5,800.

The comparatively modest value with similar structure results from the choice of wood. Ash is not as much in demand for Biedermeier furniture as the traditional woods.

382 Corner Cabinet. *Open space flanked by scrolls between bowed, double-doored bottom and corresponding glazed top. Flamed birch. 215 x 110 x 80 cm.*
North German, circa 1825. $5,000-5,800.

383 Corner Cabinet *with cutout base and gable. Mahogany. Height 210 cm.*
North German, circa 1835-40. $3,500-4,300.

Bottom and gable with the flowing lines characteristic of the late phase.

384 Corner Cabinet. *Rounded lower part with extending corners and one door. Corresponding, slightly inset top section with glazed front and flat gable.*
Mahogany. 203 x 110 x 68 cm.
North German, circa 1825. $3,000-4,000

385   386   387

385 Corner Cabinet. Angled body with glazed framed door.
Cherry, with black painted stripes on the frame. 176 x 98 x 57
cm.
South German, circa 1825. $2,700-3,200.

386 Corner Cabinet. Body with one door, glazed on three sides,
resting on tapered square legs. Needs restoration.
Cherry, partly painted black. 156 x 106 x 60 cm.
Circa 1825-30. $2,500-3,500.

387 Corner Cabinet. Glazed on three sides, with mirror on back
wall. Two bottom drawers. Needs restoration.
Walnut. 156 x 90 x 47 cm.
Circa 1825. $2,800-5000 DM

388 Corner Cabinet on shaped base. Glazed framed door and
overhanging top with cornices.
Mahogany. 141 x 93 x 57 cm.
North German, circa 1835-40. $1,800-2,400.

*The clearly recognizable curved moulding in the door frame
and drawer are typical of the late phase.*

388

389

390

391

392

Beds

389 Pair of Beds. *Foot- and head-boards with decorative braces and round bar on curved top. Cherry, panels of burled olive. 200 x 94 x 84 cm.*
South German, circa 1825. $3,500-4,500.

390 Child's Bed *with two bottom drawers and black polished half-columns on feet with rollers. Bowed, decorative railings on the movable side panels.*
Walnut. 91 x 115 x 58 cm.
South German, circa 1820-25. $2,500-3,500.

Cradle

391 Child's Cradle. *Between two round columns crowned by swans with outspread wings, the rocking cradle with its delicate carved decorations is hung.*
Cherry. Length 120 cm.
South German, circa 1820. $6,000-8,000.

Biedermeier concepts of form and choice of wood are clear here on a piece of furniture decorated in late Empire style.

Flower Gondola

392 Flower Gondola *with floral inlays and removable zinc linings. Supporting substructure on rollers.*
Mahogany. 86 x 110 x 58.5 cm.
North German, circa 1820. $4,200-5,000.

Outstanding handiwork, and a lovely example of the flower-loving Biedermeier era.

Chandeliers

393 Chandelier, *with twelve candles, delicate floral ornamentation on the ribbed dish. Gilded wood and molded composition. Electrified. Circa 1815. $5,200-6,500.*

In the production of richly ornamented chandeliers, the use of three-dimensional molded material was handy. They were made of a mixture of sawdust or scrap paper and various binding materials which hardened in air and then were gilded or bronzed.

394 Chandelier, *with ten candles, five original link chains to the hanging crown.*
Wood and other materials, gilded. Electrified. Circa 1815. $4,500-5,500.

395 Chandelier, *with twelve candles, fanlike, finely decorated dish with rows of pearl ornaments.*
Wood and other pressed materials, gilded. Circa 1815. $5,500-6,500.

393

394

395

396

397

398

Pianos

396 Hammer or spinet piano. *Keyboard on the left side, covering 4.75 octaves. Lower keys painted black, upper ones ivory-covered.*
Cherry, with dark inlaid bands. 88 x 130 x 54 cm.
South German, circa 1820-25. $4,000-4,800.

397 Spinet piano, *signed A. Kulmbach. Friedrich August Kulmbach (7/21/1803, Heilbronn-3/17/1856, Heilbronn) and his brother Wilhelm Kulmbach (3/23/1790-12/17/1855) are cited as instrument makers in the directories of the time.*
Walnut.
Heilbronn, circa 1825. $6,000-8,000.

398 Wall Piano. *Resonating chamber in lyre form, with green velvet on panel.*
Mahogany. 206 x 114 x 58 cm.
Circa 1820. $4,500-5,400

The values of Biedermeier pianos, including grand pianos, is particularly dependent, in addition to their formal design, on whether they can be played and tuned, since the required overhauling often turns out to be very expensive.

399

Miniature Furniture

Miniature furniture was made both as models and also, in more simplified form, as children's playthings.

from left to right:
399 Miniature Fireplace Screen, with embroidered picture.
Cherry. Height 40 cm.
Circa 1825. $550-675.

Miniature Chest of Drawers, with three drawers, bone knobs.
Cherry. Height 20 cm.
Circa 1820-25 $1000-1,200.

Miniature Cylinder Secretary. Bone knobs.
Mahogany. Height 29 cm.
Circa 1835. $1,800-2,400.

400 Miniature Cabinet, with one recessed paneled door.
Walnut, fir and birch. 37 x 47 x 21 cm.
Circa 1825. $675-1,000.

401 Miniature Showcase. Walnut. 47 x 32 x 15 cm.
Circa 1830. $550-800.

400

401

402

403

404

405

406

407

402 Miniature Chest of Drawers. *Two drawers flanked by half-columns, slightly projecting top drawer.*
Walnut. 26.5 x 33.5 x 21.5 cm.
Circa 1820-25. $1,800-2,500.

403 Miniature Chest of Drawers *with polished black half-columns.*
Cherry. 31 x 40 x 26 cm.
Circa 1825. $1,800-2,400.

404 Miniature Chest of Drawers *with rounded corners.*
Walnut. 34 x 32 x 19 cm.
Circa 1835. $450-675.

405 Miniature Chest of Drawers, *with two drawers and pointed feet.*
Cherry. 26 x 28.5 x 19 cm. $1,200-1,800.

406 Jewelry Box *with tapered body and high arched, slightly overhanging, hinged lid.*
Mahogany. 33 x 44 x 25 cm.
Circa 1835. $550-675.

407 Jewelry Box, *with mirror inside hinged lid, removable inner tray, two secret compartments.*
Walnut. 15 x 34 x 24 cm.
Circa 1835. $475-675.

408

409

410   411   412

408 Child's Writing Cabinet. *Classic front arrangement, slightly recessed, multi-stepped, one-drawer top.*
Walnut. Height about 150 cm.
North German-Berlin, circa 1820-25. $10,000-12,000.

Children's furniture shows the same elaborate forms and decorations as full size furniture; it is extremely rare.

409 Child's Sofa *on scroll feet.*
Walnut. Length 183 cm.
Circa 1820-25. $2,400-3,000.

410 Child's Armchair *on tapering feet, with curved back and slightly splayed armrests.*
Beech. Height 57 cm.
South German, circa 1830. $550-675.

411 Child's Chair. *Bowed rear frame with straight splats.*
Walnut. Height 60 cm.
Circa 1825. $350-475.

412 Child's Chair. *Slightly tilted back with curved boards.*
Cherry. Height 60 cm.
South German, circa 1835. $275-400.

413

414

415

Fire Screens

413 Fire Screen on rollers. Original picture in "gros-point" and "petit-point" embroidery.
Walnut. 130 x 77 cm.
Circa 1820. $2,000-2,700.

414 Fire Screen. Screen with excellent picture of a flower bouquet in "gros-point" embroidery.
Walnut. 151 x 81 cm.
Circa 1825. $1,800-2,400.

Music Stand
415 Music Stand. Two lyre-shaped sides on bowed square feet carry the tilted top.
Cherry, massive. 102 x 75 x 52 cm.
Southwest Germany, circa 1825. $2,400-3,000.

416

417

Mirrors

416 Standing Mirror, *so-called Psyche. Swinging rectangular mirror hung between two columns. Flat gable on top set off by a frieze of leaves.*
Birch. Height 192 cm.
Circa 1820-25. $2,400-3,000.

A "Psyche" is a free-standing framed structure with a large swinging mirror hung in it. This type of mirror was widespread in the Empire and Biedermeier eras.

417 Mirror. *Straight frame with polished black panels and fine decorations of stamped sheet brass.*
Cherry. Veneer damage. 153 x 79 cm.
Circa 1820. $1400-2,000.

This relatively high and narrow type of mirror is also called a pillar mirror. It was hung directly, or at just a little distance, over chests of drawers or consoles, especially in the open wall space between two windows.

418 Mirror. *In the upper panel is a round arch with a finely cut decorative mirror, showing a Rococo cavalier and a bird of paradise surrounded by floral and ornamental decor.*
Walnut. 137 x 70 cm.
Circa 1820. $1,500-2,100.

418

The quality of the cut decorative mirror is reminiscent of similar work on the very popular glass tableware of the Biedermeier era.

419

420

421

419 Mirror *with a scrolled arch. In the upper panel is a reverse painted glass panel with an allegorical motif.*
Mahogany. 166 x 60 cm.
Circa 1830. $1,500-2,000.

420 Pair of Mirrors*. In the upper panel is a glass-covered oval medallion with an allegorical figure in gilded relief carving.*
Cherry. 133 x 58 cm.
Circa 1820. $3,500-4,000.

421 Mirror*. Divided mirror surface, with flanking scrollwork above. The top board includes a node and gilded knobs.*
Mahogany. 95 x 42 cm.
North German, circa 1830. $1,000-1,500.

422

423

424

422 Mirror with blocked and molded frame.
Cherry. 117 x 57 cm.
Circa 1825. $1,200-1,500.

423 Mirror with flanking pilasters.
Walnut. 102 x 75 cm.
Circa 1825. $1,200-1,800.

424 Mirror with scalloped arch and flanking twisted columns.
Birch. 114 x 52 cm.
Circa 1835-40. $675-800.
The twisted columns and top arch indicate the late time of origin.

425 Toilette Mirror. *One-drawer in the base, with a turning oval*
mirror hung in it.
Cherry. Height 76 cm.
Circa 1820-25. $400-800.

425

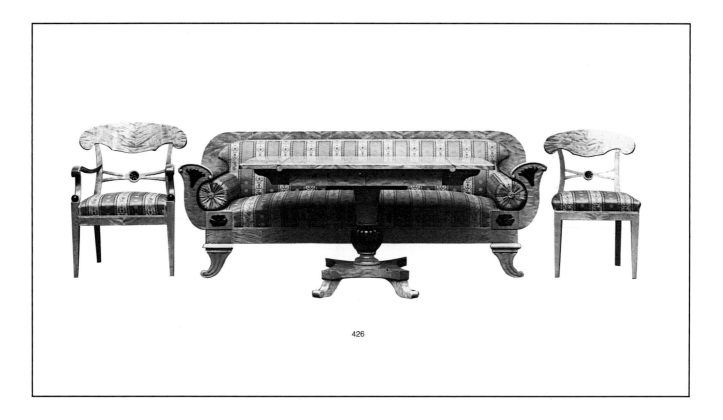

426

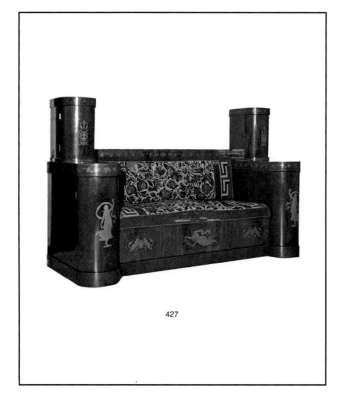

427

Later Furniture

426 Living-Room Set. *Consists of sofa, table, pair of armchairs and pair of side chairs.*
Birch.
Scandinavian-Swedish, circa 1900. $5,500-6,500.

427 Magazine Sofa. *Two one-doored side cabinets, curved in front, with corresponding upper sections flanking the sitting area, plus allegorical figures and ornamental decor added in maple.*
Mahogany.
North German, circa 1900 $2,400-3,500.

Along with the style of work, it is above all the ornamental inlays and the figures, their playful fluidity typical of Art Nouveau, that mark this original piece of furniture.

428 Living-Room Furniture. *Consists of showcase, lady's desk, table, sofa, wing chair, two bergères and two chairs. The lady's desk closely resembles a design for a piece by Josef Danhauser, formerly owned by Archduchess Sophie and now at the Austrian Museum of Commercial Art.*
Birch with ornamental inlays set off in black.
Circa 1900. $18,000-24,000.

Rare complete set, justifying an unusually high price for out of period furniture.

428

428a

428b

Bibliography

Bahns, Jörn, Biedermeier-Möbel, Entstehung—Zentren--Typen, *Munich, 1979.*

Bangert, Albrecht, Kleinmöbel aus drei Jahrhunderten, Typen—Stile—Meister, *Munich, 1978.*

Bauer, M., Märker, P., and Ohm, A., Europäische Möbel von der Gotik bis zum Jugendstil, *2nd ed., Frankfurt, 1981.*

Boehmer, Günter, Bilderbogen aus dem Biedermeier, *Munich, 1961.*

———, Die Welt des Biedermeier, *Munich, 1968.*

Boehn, Max von, Biedermeier, *Berlin, 1911.*

Christiani, Franz-Joseph, Schreibmöbelentwürfe zu Meisterstücken Braunschweiger Tischlermeister aus der 1. Hälfte des 19. Jahrhunderts, *Braunschweig 1979.*

Dewiel, Lydia, Möbel Stilkunde, Europäische Möbel aus acht Jahrhunderten, *Munich, 1980.*

Doderer, O., Biedermeier, *Mannheim, 1958.*

Eckstein, Hans, Der Stuhl, Funktion—Konstruktion—Form, *Munich, 1977.*

Egger, Gerhart, Beschläge und Schlösser an alten Möbeln, *2nd ed., Munich, 1977.*

Egger, Hanna, Herrn Biedermeiers Wunschbild, *Exhibition Catalog of the Austrian Museum of Commercial Art, Vienna, 1978.*

Exhibition Catalog, Kunsthalle Bremen, Biedermeier, *Bremen, 1967.*

Folnesics, Joseph, Innenräume und Hausrat der Empire- und Biedermeierzeit in Österreich-Ungarn, *Vienna, 1917.*

Geismeier, Willi, Biedermeier, *Leipzig, 1919.*

Gloag, Julian, A Short Dictionary of Furniture, *London, 1969.*

Haaff, Rainer, Das süddeutsche Biedermeier, *Westheim, 1991.*

Hart, H., Chairs, *New York, 1877.*

Hauser/Ostendorf, Biedermeiermöbel in Westfalen entdeckt, *Warendorf, 1990.*

Hayward. Helena, World Furniture, *London, 1965.*

Hermann, G., Das Biedermeier im Spiegel seiner Zeit, *Oldenburg/Hamburg, 1965.*

Himmelheber, Georg, Kunst des Biedermeier 1815-1835, *Munich, 1988.*

———, Historismus, Jugendstil, *Munich, 1973.*

———, Biedermeiermöbel, *Düsseldorf, 1978.*

Hirth, G., Das deutsche Zimmer, *Munich & Leipzig, 1886.*

Holm, Edith, Stühle. Von der Antike bis zur Moderne, *Munich, 1978.*

Kalkschmidt, Eugen, Biedermeiers Glück und Ende, *Munich, 1957.*

Katalog Niederösterreichischer Ausstellungsverein: Biedermeier-Ausstellung, *Vienna, 1962.*

Klatt, Erich, Konstruktion alter Möbel, *Stuttgart, 1977.*

Kreisel, Heinrich, and Himmelheber, Georg, Die Kunst des deutschen Möbels, Vol. 3, Klassizismus - Historismus - Jugendstil, *Munich, 1973.*

Krüger, Renate, Biedermeier—Eine Lebenshaltung, *Vienna, 1979.*

Luthmer, F., Deutsche Möbel der Vergangenheit, *Monographs of the Art Society, Leipzig.*

Lux, Josef August, Empire und Biedermeier, *Stuttgart, 1930.*

Meister, Peter W., and Jedding, Hermann, Das schöne Möbel im Lauf der Jahrhunderte, *Munich, 1966.*

Meyer, A. G., and Graul, R., Tafeln zur Geschichte der Möbelformen, *Leipzig, 1902-1920.*

Müller-Christensen, Sigrid, Alte Möbel vom Mittelalter bis zum Jugendstil, *7th ed., Munich, 1968.*

Museum für Kunsthandwerk: Möbelbuch, *Frankfurt am Main, 1977.*

Nagel, Gert K., Möbel, *Battenberg Antiquitäten- Katalog, Augsburg, 1994.*

Ohm, Annaliese, Möbel, *Museum für Kunsthandwerk, Frankfurt am Main, no date.*

Ottomeyer, Hans, Zopf- und Biedermeiermöbel, *Munich, 1990.*

———, Biedermeiers Glück und Ende . . . die gestörte Idylle 1815 bis 1848, *Munich, 1987.*

Ottomeyer/Schlapka, Biedermeier, *Munich, 1991.*

Pauls, Eilh. Erich, Das politische Biedermeier, *Lübeck, 1925.*

Schmidt, Robert, Möbel, *Bibliothek für Kunst- und Antiquitätensammler, 4th ed., Berlin, 1920.*

Schmitz, Hermann, Das Möbelwerk, *Berlin, 1942, and Tübingen, 1963.*

Schwarze, Wolfgang, Antike deutsche Möbel, *2nd ed., Wuppertal, 1977.*

Suppan, Martin, Biedermeier-Schreibmöbel, *Vienna, 1987.*

Ungern-Sternberg, A. von, Erinnerungsblätter aus der Biedermeier-Zeit, *Potsdam, 1919.*

Voltz, Johann Michael, Bilder aus dem Biedermeier, *Baden-Baden, 1957.*

Wiese, Wolfgang, Johannes Klinckerfuss, *Sigmaringen, 1988.*

Wilkie, Angus, Biedermeier, *New York, 1992.*

Wirth, Irmgard, Berliner Biedermeier, *Berlin, 1972.*

Zahn, E., Das fragwürdige Idyll, *Stuttgart, 1967 (radio broadcast).*

Zinnkann, Heidrun, Mainzer Möbelschreiner der ersten Hälfte des 19. Jahrhunderts, *Frankfurt am Main, 1985.*

Zweig, Marianne, Zweites Rokoko, *Vienna, 1924.*

Ziegenhorn & Jucker Hoflieferanten, Rückblick auf die historischen Möbelformen im Zusammenhang mit der modernen Raumkunst, *Erfurt, no date.*

Photo Credits

The following firms and institutions kindly placed photographic material at our disposal:
[st1hi]Alt Buchhorn firm, Elmer Reisch, Meersburgerstrasse 24, 88048 Friedrichshafen, # 397.
Auktionshaus Schloss Ahlden GmbH, 19623 Ahlden/Aller, Germany, # 4, 6, 60, 68, 113, 122, 125, 151, 197, 301, 333, 392.
Auktionshaus Arnold, Bleichstrasse 42, 60313 Frankfurt am Main, # 26, 44, 57, 177, 234, 364.
Auktionshaus August Bödiger, Franziskanerstrasse 17-19, 53113 Bonn, # 55, 174, 195, 198, 210, 219, 324.
Auktionshaus Bolland & Marotz, Fedelhören 92, 28203 Bremen, # 39, 45, 58, 224, 230, 278, 288.
Auktionshaus Leo Spik KG, Kurfürstendamm 66, 10707 Berlin, # 5, 127, 129, 133, 134.
Horst Bock, Am Löwental 48, 45239 Essen-Werden, # 427.
Braunschweig City Archives, City Museum, Braunschweig, Am Löwenwall, 38100 Braunschweig, p. 32.
Galerie Peter Griebert, Ricarda-Huch-Strasse 4, 82031 Grünwald, p. 8.
Historisches Museum, Saalgasse 19, 60331 Frankfurt am Main, p.99.
Barbara Gräfin Kayserlingk, Uerdingerstrasse 295, 47800 Krefeld, color # 24-26.
Kunsthaus am Museum, Carola von Ham, Drususgasse 1-5, 50667 Cologne, # 7, 8, 10, 14, 17, 21, 28, 74-76, 103, 105, 109,
120, 130, 132, 168, 173, 196, 227, 257, 292, 293, 295, 323, 327, 330, 331, 334, 337, 339, 352, 356, 366, 375, 402, 405, 416,419.
Märkisches Museum, Am Köllnischen Park 5, 10179 Berlin, p.23. Möller-Antik firm, Bunsenstrasse 9, 74915 Waibstadt, p. 28, # 166, 268, 272, 413, 425.
Rudolf Neumeister, Kunstauktionshaus, Barerstrasse 37, 80799 Munich (photos by Himpsl), # 9, 35, 56, 149, 150, 153, 161, 188, 190-193, 199, 225, 244, 246, 273, 275, 281, 313, 326, 335, 338, 359, 373, 398.
Arne Bruun Rasmussen Auction House, Bredgade 33, 1260 Copenhagen, Denmark, # 95, 126, 287.
Ritter Antik (Heinrich Leichter), Fahrgasse 26, 60311 Frankfurt am Main, color # 33.
Axel Schlapka, Gabelsbergerstrasse 9, 80333 Munich, color # 11, 21, 39.
Sotheby's, Steinlestrasse 7, 60596 Frankfurt am Main, color # 32.
Karin Streminski, Antiquitäten, Friesenstrasse 35, 50670 Cologne, color # 20.
Wallraf-Richartz-Museum, An der Rechtsschule, 50667 Cologne, p. 72.
All other photos were made available by the Kunstauktionshaus of Dr. Fritz Nagel, Adlerstrasse 31-33, 70199 Stuttgart.